18.95

Health and Medicine in the Christian Science Tradition

Health/Medicine and the Faith Traditions

Edited by James P. Wind

Health/Medicine and the Faith Traditions
explores the ways in which major religions
relate to the questions of human well-being.
It issues from Project Ten, an interfaith program
of The Park Ridge Center, an Institute for the Study of
Health, Faith, and Ethics.

Barbara Hofmaier, Publications Coordinator

The Park Ridge Center
is part of the Lutheran General Health Care System

The Park Ridge Center
1875 Dempster Street, Suite 175
Park Ridge, Illinois, 60068

Health and Medicine in the Christian Science Tradition

PRINCIPLE, PRACTICE, AND CHALLENGE

Robert Peel

Crossroad • New York

1989

The Crossroad Publishing Company
370 Lexington Avenue, New York, N.Y. 10017

Printed in the United States of America

Library of Congress Cataloging-in-Publication Data

Peel, Robert, 1909–
  Health and medicine in the Christian Science tradition :
  principle, practice, and challenge / Robert Peel.
  p.   cm. — (Health/medicine and the faith traditions)
  Includes index.
  ISBN 0-8245-0895-5 :
  1. Health—Religious aspects—Christian Science.   2. Medicine-
  -Religious aspects—Christian Science.   3. Christian Science-
  -Doctrines.   I. Title.   II. Series.
  [DNLM: 1. Christian Science.   2. Mental Healing.   3. Religion and
  Medicine.   WB 885 P374h]
  BX6950.P44   1988
  261.5′6—dc19
  DNLM/DLC
  for Library of Congress   88-20266
                                                                       CIP

Contents

Foreword

The Christian Scientist who reads this book will experience the familiar, the familiar better explained and detailed here than elsewhere. Robert Peel is certainly a veteran well qualified to present Christian Science to those who practice that faith.

The non–Christian Scientist who reads this book will experience the unfamiliar, the unfamiliar better brought home and examined here than elsewhere. It is hard to picture citizens who do not have, or who cannot quickly acquire, curiosity about their Christian Scientist neighbors. Such readers may have walked around for years with bits of information and pieces of misinformation overbalanced by unsatisfied curiosity about these neighbors, their beliefs, their practices. Robert Peel is, to our knowledge, the most capable introducer of this faith, the one who best anticipates the questions one would have. This is the sixth of the books in this series that I have introduced through a foreword, and at least five more such assignments lie ahead. Some of these books dealt with the medical and religious worlds of spiritual siblings, thought worlds with which I felt immediate relationship: the next-of-kin worlds of Reformed, Catholic, Methodist, and Anglican Christianity. It did not greatly stretch experience to be at home with Judaism. Even Islam, a world that I find alluring and forbidding at once, represented the more or less easily comprehensible. A conventional Christian or Jew has little difficulty knowing why Muslims do what they do and believe what they believe.

Not so with Christian Science, whose world, even after Robert Peel is finished building bridges, still seems a figurative faraway place. The members of the Church of Christ, Scientist, seem very much at home in "my" world. They balance accounts, enjoy good food, travel in cars and planes with the rest of us (I've often looked over the shoulder to see a fellow passenger on a jet reading *Science and Health with Key to the Scriptures*). Yet when it comes to the world of clinics and hospitals, pharmacies and medical schools and laboratories, they hold back. They may express criticisms, even rejections, of "my" world of medical-religious meanings. The transformations they suggest strike me as curious and perhaps at times threatening.

So threatening, says Peel—and I had not known this—that legislative activity calling into question Christian Science practice has been growing, not declining, since about 1974. What Christian Scientists regard as their religious liberty is being inhibited by citizens who are moving through congresses and courts to impose technological medicine on people who do not think they should be judged for the healing they bring—or for the occasional failures.

Such a beguiling, confusing, and threatening world requires exposition of the sort Robert Peel provides. Some readers may be momentarily puzzled by the genre. The collection of "testimonies" Peel advances departs from the usual form of substantiating scholarly writing. But that aspect of this medium is the message. Christian Science will always find itself a minority voice, arcane sounding, among the voices that dominate in a culture. Although it has established itself as a very respectable element in the citizenry, these pages testify that Christian Science is also always on trial, always explaining itself, always finding it important to commend its own ways. This is done here as elsewhere without a spirit of proselytism, proselytism having been forbidden by Mary Baker Eddy, the "discoverer" of Christian Science. Yet there is here a self-conscious presentation of the Christian Scientist self and world.

If reasons exist for defensiveness, for seizing occasions to explain oneself, reasons also exist for seeing these habits as intrinsic to the character of Christian Science. If not proselytizing or missionary, if never aggressive or belligerent—when did a Christian Scientist ever jam a tract at you or mobilize an army?—it is always quietly setting out to revise or correct the settled world views that others take so for granted. Members of that faith tradition have serene confidence that, no matter what the numbers, the prejudices, the ignorance "out there" that impinge on their small group, they are standing where the light of Truth falls, and they like it if others stand there too.

Along the way, using the "testimonies" method to bring an immediacy that not all books in series like this can have, Peel provides a great deal of information. He makes many connections between what for most of us is the little bit already known and the great amount we need to learn. It is very much a part of his vision, as is true for other scholars from within the tradition, to show the compatibility of Christian Science with mainstream ways, the ties it has to religions we have already found familiar.

In the age after the hippies, in a culture where there are kooks, scholars of Christian Science want to show how nonkooky is their world view and how legitimate are Christian Science practices. Mary Baker Eddy, in these pages as in Peel's three-volume biography, culturally represents an element in the New England Puritan tradition which does not have to explain itself to the neighbors. Although this faith, with its radical spirituality, contains real challenges to "orthodox" Christianity, there are also more points of contact than one might previously have guessed.

Embarrassing things can of course be said about this tradition, as about all others. There are no easy ways to understand it or practice it. Peel makes clear the hard choices so that readers know the spiritual, moral, and intellectual expense, as it were, that members invest before they get a commensurate yield. This is not a "Ten Easy Steps" religion that one picks up as easily as one breezes through the latest health-and-religion best-seller from airport newsstands.

This series on health and medicine in the faith traditions has a double focus. Each book should offer the members of that tradition a larger repertory of options and understandings, greater resources for times of crisis and for the fulfilling of responsibilities. At the same time, nonmembers will learn about their neighbors' and fellow-citizens' worlds. They may borrow insight even as they grow in sympathy.

We frequently advertise the relevance of the books to health care professionals who serve patients in these faith traditions. Christian Scientists, however, are supposed to be meeting their needs away from the clinic. Yet it is true, as Peel recognizes, that many members of the Church of Christ, Scientist, do find reason to come into contact with clinic and clinician. Because such persons live in the borderland between two often apparently incompatible worlds, they and those who would care for them need help of the sort Peel's information and perspective impart. Most of the time, however, the contacts will occur far from the clinic, in realms of thought and human contact which always can stand some enhancement. Peel's book, I believe, is an enhancer.

Martin E. Marty

Introduction

Can one actually speak of a Christian Science "tradition"?

In other words, does a religious movement organized little more than one hundred years ago merit a term that suggests the collective persistence of a unique set of fundamental spiritual values through many generations of change and challenge?

The answer may be, in part, that the changes in society during the past one hundred years have been more radical than in the entire four hundred years preceding them. Today Christian tradition in all its varied manifestations faces a profounder challenge to its continued existence than at any time since the advent of Christianity. For a newborn nineteenth-century church to hold its original purpose through the incredible scientific and psychological revolution of this past century—not to mention the quantum leap of biomedicine in the past half century—is a miracle in itself. Perhaps fifth-generation members of such a church may justly speak of their religious tradition.

However, to many Christian Scientists the term carries a much deeper implication than one hundred years of denominational history. In their view, the roots of their faith extend to the first century, not just to the nineteenth.

It was in 1879 that a small group of evangelical New Englanders formed the Church of Christ, Scientist. Under the leadership of Mary Baker Eddy, the then little-known author of a book provocatively entitled (in its final form) *Science and Health with Key to the Scriptures*, they voted to "organize a church designed to commemorate the word and works of our Master, which should reinstate primitive Christianity and its lost element of healing."[1]

1

This was by no means the only group in nineteenth-century America that aspired to restore the pristine purity of New Testament Christianity. In new and old denominations there were evidences of a desire to recapture what was taken to be the nonritualistic, nondogmatic, nonhierarchic simplicity and spiritual fellowship of the Apostolic Age. The Disciples of Christ, the Holiness sects emerging from Methodism, the New Light Presbyterians of Kentucky, the Come-outers from Cape Cod, the Quakers, Shakers, and Swedenborgians from earlier periods, the Universalists and transcendentalized liberals like Theodore Parker and Cyrus Bartol—all these and others were touched in one way or another by a yearning for the spirit of primitive Christianity.

In the case of Christian Science this yearning was united with a strong emphasis on the renewal of Christian healing. Here was a tradition rooted in the New Testament itself, yet almost disappearing through long periods of subsequent church history. The late nineteenth century saw a revival of spiritual healing by the Pentecostals and the remarkable healing work of Pastor Johann Christoph Blumhardt in Germany, not to mention the much-disputed miracles at Lourdes. But in none of these did the healing activity play such a central role as in Christian Science—or offer such a direct challenge to both the religious and the medical orthodoxy of the day.

Nevertheless, it is only in the long tradition of Christian healing and New Testament interpretation that Christian Science can be properly understood. Its healing is literally inseparable from its theology. Its "medicine," Eddy wrote, is "Mind."[2] And by capitalizing that word, the founder of the Church of Christ, Scientist, indicated that she was referring not to the fallible human mind but to what St. Paul called "the mind of Christ," that is, the infinite, divine Mind commonly called God and habitually addressed by Jesus as a loving Father, the very ground of his being and the fountainhead of his healing and saving power.

On the other hand, the Christian Science tradition does have unique features that distinguish it from the modern upsurge of religious or faith healing in the traditional churches. While Eddy's perception of God as Principle, of Christianity as science, of Spirit as substance, and of grace as law has some surprising verbal affinities with the classical formulations of the metaphysics of Thomas Aquinas and Jonathan Edwards, it has an alarmingly unorthodox tone to many Christian ears. And of course, in our age of scientific skepticism, radical empiricism, pragmatic relativism, and technocratic imperialism, metaphysics until very recently has seemed—even to many theologians—an ignominious retreat from reality to outmoded god-language games.

Science, as generally understood today, cannot lean on tradition in the same way theology does. By its very nature science is antihistorical. Its past is strewn with discarded "certainties." Its current principles, theories, and methodologies, amazingly fruitful as they may be, must by its own rigorous logic remain open to the constant possibility of modification or rejection, as new discoveries compel new tests, new hypotheses, new modes of thinking. While its human practitioners may sometimes speak with unwarranted dogmatism, the scientific enterprise as such has no place for dogmas of any kind. Hence the continuing tensions between science and religious orthodoxy.

This is evident not merely on the fundamentalist front, but also in more subtle areas of thought, faith, and ethics. Earlier volumes in this series have already shown the rich diversity of the approaches made by faith traditions to the subject of health and medicine. While seeking common ground between healing as science or technology and healing as spiritual reconciliation and wholeness, each tradition has its own emphases, its own special contribution to a debate likely to continue for many, many years.

Because Christian Science is much less familiar than the older faith traditions to most readers, I devote Chapters 1 and 2 to clarifying the faith's widely misunderstood genesis and metaphysics. Only so can the rest of the book treat meaningfully the specific questions suggested for the series as a whole.

"In the beginning, God . . ." is still the keystone of the Judeo-Christian tradition. In that respect Christian Science is entirely orthodox. We must begin at the beginning.

·1·
Christian Science: Theology or Therapy?

In my beginning is my end. . . .
In my end is my beginning.
—T. S. Eliot, Four Quartets

The official date for Mary Baker Eddy's "discovery" of Christian Science is 1866, but its beginnings go back further than that. In her autobiographical sketch *Retrospection and Introspection* she would later write, "During twenty years prior to my discovery I had been trying to trace all physical effects to a mental cause."[1] A hint of this appears in an article on the immortality of the soul which she wrote for an obscure journal almost exactly twenty years earlier. At the time, she was a young widow living in a remote New Hampshire village, burdened with wretched health and wholly without means of her own. The article reads in part:

> Who does not sometimes conjecture what will be his condition and employment in eternity? Will the mind be continually augmenting its stock of knowledge, and advancing toward complete perfection? It cannot be otherwise.
> We shall there apprehend fully the relations and dependencies incomprehensible to understandings encircled by clay. The boundless ocean of truth will be fathomed and investigated by those, whom, like Newton, a residence here scarcely acquainted with a few pebbles on its trackless shore. The result of all experiments will then be satisfactory, since they will accord with the deductions of enlarged and enlightened reason.
> Most authors have but dimly shadowed forth their own imaginings, and much of what they intended is involved in obscurity. This makes an approach to the regions of science and literature so extremely difficult; there this obstacle will be removed. No veil will hide from our observation

the beauties, lovely, inimitable, of wisdom and philosophy; all their charms will there be displayed.

The imperfection of language will be no hindrance to the acquisition of ideas, as it will no longer be necessary as a medium of thought and communication. Intelligence, refined, etherealized, will converse directly with material objects, *if, indeed, matter be existent. . . .* (Emphasis added)[2]

The last clause might be taken as merely a whiff of philosophical idealism, caught perhaps from Emerson who had written only the year before, "Intellectual science has been observed to beget invariably a doubt of the existence of matter," and gone on to quote Turgot's statement: "He that has never doubted the existence of matter, may be assured he has no aptitude for metaphysical inquiries."[3]

But the young widow's doubts had deeper roots than philosophical speculation. She herself wrote later of the "hunger and thirst after divine things" that she had had from childhood—her deep desire "for something higher and better than matter, and apart from it."[4] There is a good deal of evidence to support this claim, though it has been largely ignored by her critics. However, one of the more acid of them, the English historian H. A. L. Fisher, despite his generally supercilious approach to Christian Science, had the grace to acknowledge and the acumen to define (with unusual precision) the religious impulse in Eddy's early life:

If the metaphysical promptings of her mind impelled her to search for a system of the universe, the religious side of it gave to that system its emotional quality and content. Prayer, meditation, eager and puzzled interrogation of the Bible, had claimed from childhood much of her energy, so that those who met her in later times were conscious of a certain quiet exaltation, such as may come to a woman nursing a secret spiritual advantage. . . . When we ask what was the inner source of her power, the answer can only be that it was religion. . . . The great ideas of God, of immortality, of the soul, of a life penetrated by Christianity, were never far from her mind.[5]

At the same time Eddy rebelled early against the doctrine of predestination in the Edwardsian "New Light Calvinism" of her family and pastors. Later she rebelled also against the pious ideal of Christian resignation to the ills and sufferings supposedly imposed by God on human beings for the betterment of their souls. She had good reason to do so, as the first half of her long life had a great deal more bodily illness and pain than could be readily squared with the loving, purposeful God revealed through Jesus.

The root trouble, according to her doctors, was "spinal inflammation," accompanied by acute dyspepsia and assorted gastrointestinal disorders. A more careful recent study of her various symptoms as described in the Baker family correspondence points strongly to inflammation of the gall bladder as probably the basic affliction. Whatever the medical verdict, the result in Mary Baker's life was that her search for a more deeply satisfying theodicy was intertwined with her long search for health.

This latter quest turned out to be a disappointing trek through the wilds of mid-century allopathy, hydropathy, homeopathy, mesmerism, the Graham system of Spartan diet, and the suggestive therapeutics of the ex-mesmerist Phineas P. Quimby of Portland, Maine. Apart from the deep solace of the Bible, the only bright spots in those weary years were what she learned from homeopathy and Quimbyism.

From her own homeopathic experiments with drugs diluted to the vanishing point, then carried on with sugar-pill placebos, she came to the conclusion that the patient's mental attitudes and faith were the potent elements in drug therapy. Quimby, who brought about what seemed for a short time to be a final cure of her long-standing illness, strengthened this conviction by his theory that disease itself is primarily a mental phenomenon.

In order to connect with the thinking of his patients, most of whom had simple evangelical backgrounds, Quimby tried to link his mind-cure with the healings of Jesus, as other backwoods healers taking off from animal magnetism (mesmerism) also tended to do. One of these, Warren Felt Evans, a Methodist minister turned Swedenborgian, visited Quimby twice between 1863 and 1866, discovered that their methods were very similar, and in 1872 in a book entitled *Mental Medicine* paid brief tribute to the Portland healer who, he said, had "seemed to reproduce the wonders of the Gospel history." But, he added, "all this was only an exhibition of the force of suggestion, or the action of the law of faith, over a patient in the impressible condition." Significantly, he defined the impressible condition as a "magnetized" state not involving the usual mesmeric sleep or trance.[6]

Eddy, agog over her temporary healing and certainly in a very impressible state of mind, was swept off her feet by Quimby's assurance that this was the very method of Jesus Christ. From the outset she appears to have ignored entirely his theory of mind as "spiritual matter," summed up in his statement: "My foundation is animal matter, or life. This, set in action by wisdom, produces thought."[7] While greatly taken with his statement that "there is no intelligence in matter," she paid no attention whatever to his definition of mind as "the fluids of the body," that is, the magnetic or "electro-nervous" fluids prominent in the literature of animal magnetism.

The paradoxical relation between the two is again caught neatly, if condescendingly, by H. A. L. Fisher. While Quimby jotted down the theories suggested by his cases, Fisher wrote, Eddy "embroidered her own reflections" on his reflections. "The gentleman," he added, "was confused; the lady was by no means clear; and the attempt to found upon the Quimby cures a philosophy of healing equally compatible with Quimby's own processes and convictions, and the very opposite religious preconceptions entertained by his lady friend and literary coadjutor, was by no means an easy task."[8]

What followed, almost predictably, is foreshadowed by a characteristic passage in an 1864 manuscript by Quimby, written after many long discussions with Eddy, whom he described to another of his patients as "a very wonderful woman":[9]

> Man, like the earth, is throwing off a vapor, and that contains his knowledge. Out of this vapor comes a more perfect identity of living matter. . . . The spiritual rib that rises from man is more perfect matter or soil, called woman. . . . I do not mean that woman means every female. Nor do I pretend to say that man means everything of the animal. But that the mind of the female contains more of that superior substance required to receive the higher development of God's wisdom. For this element is pure love. . . . It separates her from matter and brings her into that spiritual state that rises from all animal life. . . . Then she becomes a teacher of that science which puts man in possession of a wisdom that can subject all animal life to its own control . . . and man stands to woman as a servant to his Lord. . . .[10]

Years later, long after her "discovery" of Christian Science, Eddy gave her own account of her final turning away from Quimbyism:

> I tried him as a healer, and because he seemed to help me for the time, and had a higher ideal than I had heard of up to that time, I praised him to the skies . . . ; I actually loved him, I mean his high and noble character . . . but when I found that Quimbyism was too short, and would not answer the cry of the human heart for succor, for real aid, I went, being driven there by my extremity, to the Bible, and there I discovered Christian Science; and when I had found it, I deserted Quimby and his scheme of healing just as I had in turn deserted everything else . . . and I have built Christian Science upon the Petra of the Scriptures.[11]

The decisive turning point in this development appears to have been the healing of a critical injury Eddy received in 1866, shortly after Quimby's death. The healing, she explained, occurred in a moment of spiritual illumination as she read the account of one of Jesus' healings in the New Testament. "That short experience," she wrote later, "included a glimpse of the great fact that I have since tried to make plain to others, namely, Life in and of Spirit; this Life being the sole reality of existence."[12] The apparently simple phrase "sole reality" marks a crucial leap in thought from Quimby's mental probings.

To Eddy herself the experience seemed a revelation of the radical spiritual fact at the heart of Jesus' healing and teaching—or better, of his whole life. It was, she felt, a theological discovery or spiritual insight that raised Christian healing far above the psychological techniques of mind-curers like Quimby and Evans.

Her recognition of this crucial difference of approach, however, did not take place all at once. For several years as she pored over the Bible, exploring the new spiritual landscape that was opening to her thought, she hung on to some of her former mentor's concepts and terminology, as in the statement that "there is no intelligence in matter." Yet actually she meant by this something antithetical to his crude view of intelligence as seated in a mind that emanated like a mist or vapor from the physical body. Only gradually did she come to see his healing system as essentially mesmeric, the control of one human mind by another—even though Quimby was reaching out tentatively for something more spiritual at the time she knew him.

The great German church historian Karl Holl in his remarkably accurate critical analysis of Eddy's theology pointed almost casually to the key factor ignored by those who tried to put her in the line of descent from Mesmer. "That which connected her with Quimby," he wrote, "was her conviction that all disease in the last analysis has its roots in the mind, and that healing therefore must be effected through mental influence. But," he added, "it was her earnest Puritan faith in God which separated her from Quimby from the beginning." Holl again went to the heart of the matter in a one-sentence comment on Eddy's account of her 1866 healing, an account scoffed at by some critics as an obvious revision of history. "If one tries," he wrote with a slight impatience, "even for a moment, to erase this religious experience from her life as a fable invented by her later on, then her entire struggle in the following years becomes incomprehensible, especially her opposition to mesmerism."[13]

Holl, from his Lutheran standpoint, took basic issue with Eddy's theology, but he reported it understandingly and recognized it as the major force in her own life, in the movement she founded, and in the healing she taught. It is no part of the purpose of this book to defend or to interpret her theology, but it is the purpose of this chapter to make clear the centrality of Christian theology (as she understood it) in her founding of Christian Science.

It has sometimes been claimed that Eddy's basic interest was in the cure of disease, and that she later added a thin veneer of Christianity in order to give her curative system a larger public appeal. The evidence of her early manuscripts shows this to be a total misrepresentation of the facts, and it is corroborated by the firsthand testimony of those who knew her in the months following her healing in 1866.

In the latter part of that year, Eddy lived for several months in the home of a friend—a Mrs. Ellis of Swampscott, Massachusetts—and the friend's son, Fred, who was at that time the village schoolmaster. Each day she would stay in her room studying the Bible, pondering, praying, struggling to find language to express the new ideas that were flooding into her thought. In the evening, according to Fred Ellis, she would come down from her room and read to the mother and son what she had written during the day, asking for their criticisms, explaining what she meant.

Thirty-five years later, when she had become an internationally known figure, Ellis wrote her a warm but slightly awed letter, one paragraph of which recreates something of the 1866 atmosphere: "It may be presumption in me to address you. I do so, not in the light of the magnificence of your achievement, but out of my cherished remembrance of those precious evenings in the little sitting-room at Swampscott, when the words of Jesus, of Truth, were so illumined by your inspired interpretation."[14]

Eddy's first student, a young cobbler named Hiram Crafts, stated in a 1901 affidavit, "At that date [1866–67] I was a Spiritualist, but her teachings changed my views on that subject and I gave up spiritualism. . . . She taught me from the Scriptures and from manuscripts that she wrote when she taught me." In a 1902 letter he clarified this further: "We used nothing outside of the New Testament, and had no manuscripts of any kind until after I had been studying six months."[15]

Another young man, Charles Allen Taber, who came in contact with Eddy at that period through his aunt, a Mrs. Winslow, was somewhat more sophisticated in his analysis. In a 1913 affidavit he recalled the passing relationship in some detail:

> Mrs. Winslow, a broad minded and well educated member of the Society of Friends, and my wife a zealous church member, had both made a careful study of the Bible, but [Mrs. Eddy] led us toward an understanding of the Bible which neither of us had ever reached. The central principle of her conversation seemed to be the power over, the control of our

physical and mental faculties, through the study of, the belief in and the daily practice of the teachings of Christ as she understood them. We said that she was reading into the Bible more than we could find in the text, but we had to admit that her ideas had a good foundation in the Bible and in the writings of some of the greatest religious teachers of the world. She made a protest against the idea, then somewhat prevalent, that we should take but little thought as to our bodies and our earthly lives, and consider only the life to come.

The affidavit goes on to describe Eddy's letting them read the manuscript on which she was then working—a bulky document full of interlineations and verbal changes, difficult to read but evidencing her struggle to find a vocabulary in which to express her rapidly evolving thought. Taber's final comment was this: "After we had read the manuscript and were talking the matter over we realized that perhaps [Mrs. Eddy] had cognition of certain great principles in the life and teachings of Christ which were not well understood or properly set forth by religious teachers."[16]

It was as a Christian thinker, not merely an advocate of mental healing, that these people saw her. To be sure, as her reputation grew, many people did turn to Christian Science first of all for physical healing. But if they went to Eddy for instruction on *how* to heal, they found that the first three days of her teaching were devoted entirely to the question, What is God? And the answer to that question, they soon discovered, required a spiritual commitment that many of them had never dreamed of. Some found the demand too great. Others apparently felt like Saul when he went in search of his father's asses but found a kingdom instead. But no one was left with the impression that Christian Science was merely a therapeutic technique, a matter of autosuggestion, positive thinking, or mind over matter.

Then what was it?

·2·

The Word Made Flesh

John saw the human and divine coincidence, shown in the man Jesus, as divinity embracing humanity in Life and its demonstration,—reducing to human perception and understanding the Life which is God.

—Science and Health with Key to the Scriptures

In 1870 Mary Baker Eddy taught her first class on Christian Science (still embryonic) to a handful of inquirers in Lynn, Massachusetts. In the forty years that followed she reached hundreds of thousands of people, if not millions, through her writings. Along the way, rather to her surprise, she founded a new Christian denomination which by 1910 had members scattered around the world.

In 1964–65, almost one hundred years after the birth of Christian Science, several representatives of The First Church of Christ, Scientist, in Boston took part in a series of ecumenical discussions with clerical and lay leaders from two mainline denominations of the Reformed tradition. With considerable zest the Christian Scientists and the mainline church leaders explored their theological differences as well as the Christian values they shared.

One of the position papers prepared by the Christian Science representatives attracted special interest from the other participants, and a few excerpts from it may serve as a useful introduction to this chapter. Entitled "Sin and Grace," the paper leaped at once to the issue of theodicy, central to Christian Science teachings, but typically it started from a concrete example, in this case drawn from *The Education of Henry Adams*:

> It was unthinkable, Henry Adams wrote after his sister, racked with suffering, had died of tetanus, "that any personal deity could find pleasure or profit in torturing a poor woman, by accident, with a fiendish cruelty

13

known to man only in perverted and insane temperaments." Yet millions of Christians have believed traditionally in just such a God.

Cruelty, waste, indifference, and pain are inherent in the very structure and texture of the natural world. Much of this cannot easily be attributed to human wickedness. It is "natural" evil, in the common phrase, and the Christian apologist has usually explained it as the condition of man's creatureliness. In this explanation the agonies and accidents of material existence are held to be the necessary matrix of its blessings and possibilities.

But why create such a universe in the first place? Could not a perfect God create a perfectly good universe, as in the great vision of Genesis 1, where the flawless creation metaphorically presented for contemplation bears little resemblance to nature as we encounter it through the physical senses, with its ceaseless, savage struggle for existence?[1]

Are we to suppose, the paper continues, that God as the very Principle of good must share his power with an antithetical, evil force, in Manichaean fashion? Would human life be tame and ignoble without such struggles and defeats, such matter-bound limits, such engulfing mortality? Are we to believe, for instance, that Providence has arranged for a natural order which over the centuries has brought into existence "countless deformed and imbecile children, children destined to suffer hideous pain, to die of famine and accident, to be slaughtered in war or burned alive in holocaust, to have their lives distorted by inherited criminal tendencies and vicious social systems?" And then the mordant question: "Are these the children of a loving heavenly Father?"

If we ask such questions about "natural" evil, what are we to say about moral evil, or sin? If an omnipotent and omniscient God created human beings free to choose good or evil but knew from the outset that many of them would choose evil, must the creator himself not take the ultimate responsibility? To the traditional answer that permissiveness is the necessary precondition of free will and that without freedom to sin human beings would be the mere slaves or puppets of God's will, the position paper replies that true freedom is freedom to fulfill one's highest potentialities. Surely the sinner is the slave of his or her own blindness to what true spiritual being is. Is God free to sin? If the answer is no, must we then pity a deific power that is a "slave" to its own infinite goodness? The paper concludes:

The physical organism determined by chancy genes and contingent circumstance is the puppet—though not of God's will (unless one chooses to make God responsible for the worst as well as the best of human behavior). If the man of God's creating is identified with the puppet-mortal evolved from primal matter, free will becomes logically untenable and sin becomes, as in modern scientism, mere sickness and maladjustment, to be healed by social reconditioning rather than by spiritual rebirth.

This leads to the secular point of view that natural and moral evil are essentially one, capable of progressive amelioration through human ingenuity but, in the last analysis, built into the limitations of the material universe. Once again it remains an unfathomable mystery why God, as traditional Christianity maintains, should have created such a universe in the first place.

At this point Christian Science takes the position that the universe we encounter through our physical senses (and their instrumental extensions) is *not* the universe of God's creating. Genesis 1 is to be understood not as the story of a literal or physical creation but as a symbolic representation of the unfolding to finite human thought of the eternal perfection of the universe as it exists in the Mind that is God. The long agony of earthly history is not "reality" as the divine Mind knows it—except as that history registers the breakthroughs of spiritual light, great and small, awakening, redeeming, healing, transforming, and lifting thought toward the one reality: God, the All-in-all.

This view of God as All is not as far from traditional theology as some people have supposed. Properly understood, it is neither mysticism nor pantheism, any more than is Paul's statement that "in him we live, and move, and have our being." Karl Holl in his essay on Christian Science takes account of the larger ontological framework in which the subject needs to be seen when he writes:

> The statement that God is the sole reality is the basis of every true religion, not of a degenerate religion. The intellectual converse of this proposition is that the world is an illusion. The highest exponents of religion have been the very ones who have at all times touched upon this proposition. . . . [But] in order to hold onto both the reality of God and the reality of the world, explanations resort to saying that there is a higher reality above the lower, a true reality behind that of the senses, that there are stages of being, etc. Intellectual analysis shows all these explanations to be mere expedients. The concept of being eliminates gradations. A thing either is or it is not. It is either real or it is unreal.[2]

A Christian Scientist might agree that while a "thing" either is or is not, one cannot extend the statement blandly to anything so complex as the whole of human experience, in which fact and illusion, reality and unreality, truth and error, may seem hopelessly intermeshed until separated by the Holy Spirit itself—variously described as divine revelation and divine science.

The theme of God as the only reality runs through Christian history, not only in the great mystical tradition represented by Johannes Eckhart but also in the great metaphysical tradition illustrated in our time by Paul Tillich. When Tillich describes God as the ground of being or more exactly as Being itself, he adds that although this is necessarily the first statement to be made about God, it is not the last. There are, he points out, many other statements "such as God is life and love and spirit, all of which are derived from revelatory experiences, and all of which can be expressed ontologically."[3] That by no means rules out the personal encounter with God, Tillich insists, but it excludes the assertion that God is *a* person.

Half a century earlier Mary Baker Eddy had written:

> As the words *person* and *personal* are commonly and ignorantly employed, they often lead, when applied to Deity, to confused and erroneous conceptions of divinity and its distinction from humanity. If the term personality, as applied to God, means infinite personality, then God *is* infinite *Person*,—in the sense of infinite personality, but not in the lower sense.[4]

As in Eddy's day, so today all Christian Science class instruction starts with a consideration in depth of God's name and nature. This is not a gnostic imparting of a secret doctrine to a chosen elite, but a careful, reverent study of a God revealed in Scripture as spirit, life, truth, love—terms capitalized in Christian Science when used for Deity. A God to be known not only as infinite Person but also as the underlying Principle (or, as Tillich put it, the ground) of all true being. A God to be known above all else through direct encounter in daily experience.

The concept of God as Principle also has its roots in the Puritan (and especially the Edwardsian) theology in which Eddy was raised. As that preeminent historian of the New England mind, Perry Miller, has written, "'God' was a word to stand for the majesty and perfection which gleam through the fabric of the world; He was Being, hardly apprehensible to man, yet whose existence man must posit, not so much as *a* being but as *The* Being, the beginning of things and the sustainer, the principle of universal harmony."[5]

Is this a mere theological abstraction? Not for an Edwards certainly—and, in a different way, not for an Eddy. One position paper in the ecumenical series referred to above puts it this way: "As infinite Person and divine Principle, God lives and loves with the fullest intensity, caring intimately for His whole creation, with every identity precious in His sight."[6] A fine conviction, but one that needs to be put to the test in concrete experience.

Keats said it wryly: "Axioms in philosophy are not axioms until they are proved upon our pulses."[7]

C. S. Lewis in his book on miracles made a related point:

> [God] must not be thought of as a featureless generality. . . . He is the most concrete thing there is, the most individual. . . . Body and personality as we know them are the real negatives—they are what is left of positive being when it is sufficiently diluted to appear in temporal or finite forms. . . . Divine Sonship is, so to speak, the solid of which biological sonship is merely a diagrammatic representation on the flat.[8]

When the founder of Christian Science was asked in 1887 whether she believed in "infinite progression" or limitless spiritual growth after death—a question she herself had asked forty years earlier in her article on the immortality of the soul—she replied, "Infinite progression is concrete being, which finite mortals see and comprehend only as abstract glory."[9] Christian Science has always demanded that the concrete reality of spirit be proved in some measure as present fact.

Viewed from this standpoint, the scientific materialist rather than the spiritual healer is the victim of what Whitehead called "the fallacy of misplaced concreteness." Einstein's famous statement that it is "the theory that decides what we can observe" pointed to more than he anticipated. Quantum physicist Niels Bohr went on to say that even though "in our future encounters with reality we shall have to distinguish between the objective and the subjective side" of every physical process, the location of the separation "may depend upon the way things are looked at; to a certain extent it can be chosen at will."[10] It can be chosen, for instance, at a point where concrete experience appears to contradict current scientific theory.

All of which leads to the historic "scandal" of Christianity, its exclusive particularity, its rootedness in a unique event in the distant past. The rationalist philosopher examining Christianity is confronted with not a generalized argument but a special case—with a small-time healer and teacher in an obscure Roman province who both acted and spoke with amazing assurance as the Son of God. To Christian Scientists, as to all other Christians of course, Jesus the Christ stands at the center of history, the one figure who could announce with complete authority, "He that hath seen me hath seen the Father." He was, one might say, the concrete evidence of what God is—and what man and woman in reality are as the expression of God's being.

While Jesus as Savior is central to the teachings of Christian Science, the divine grace expressed through his life is not regarded as limited or personal. Instead, it is to be understood as the expression of universal and demonstrable law—"the life-giving law of the Spirit," Paul writes, which frees "from the law of sin and death" those who are "united with Christ Jesus."[11] United, perhaps, most basically in their common spiritual heritage as the sons and daughters of the infinite One—heirs of God and joint-heirs with Christ.

This emphasis on the preexistent perfection of each individual as an original expression of the divine Mind troubled Karl Holl. "The deepest thoughts of Christianity," he wrote, "are lost on a plane where man's hope is founded solely upon the fact that he is created by God." This led him to a tentative conclusion that there is no place in Christian Science for

> any religious thought which presupposes the reality of the corporeal world—the view that man has been placed by God into an order to which he has to adjust himself, the concept of suffering as a means of instruction or punishment, the thought of retributive justice by God, the duty in respect to patience, submission, humility, etc. But opposed to this we have the fact that Mrs. Eddy speaks about all these things in *Science and Health*, and in part very beautifully. It may be argued that this is only a remnant of her Christian education which could be said not to agree with her fundamental views. That may be so. But these things are to be found in the [textbook] of the Scientists and have a certain connection with its basic point of departure. Because of this they affect the practical outlook of Christian Science as well.[12]

Holl's caveat is weakened by his puzzled admission that there is after all a "certain connection" between the basic ontology of Christian Science and its view of the redemptive mission of the Christ in human experience. To explain this, he assumed that Eddy used the words *real* and *unreal* less as ontological categories than as psychological aids in the practice of spiritual healing. This missed the mark rather widely, since the reality/unreality distinction is at the very heart of Christian Science. Yet Holl was groping toward the recognition that Christian healing (of sin as well as sickness) is in fact the link between the absolute metaphysics of Christian Science and its Christian concern for baffled and suffering humankind.

This is both illustrated and summed up in a key statement from *Science and Health*, "The divinity of the Christ was made manifest in the humanity of Jesus"—a dictum amplified by a further statement from the same source:

> "The Word was made flesh." Divine Truth must be known by its effects on the body as well as on the mind, before the Science of being can be demonstrated. Hence its embodiment in the incarnate Jesus,—that life-link forming the connection through which the real reaches the unreal, Soul rebukes sense, and Truth destroys error.[13]

What Holl calls the "practical outlook" of Christian Science is reflected in the constant recurrence of the words *demonstrate* and *demonstration* in its literature. *Science and Health* even lifts these words to theological stature when it declares that "demonstration is Immanuel, or *God with us*."[14] Abstract glory, it is clear, must be demonstrated as concrete being, preexistent perfection as present redemption. Healing through prayer and spiritual commitment is more than the restoration of physical well-being; it is—to the one who experiences it, at least—an evidence or demonstration of the living presence of God and his Christ.

There is a curious parallelism here between Christian Science and the matured position of a theological giant of our age, Karl Barth. The differences between the two theologies are of course monumental, but this makes the points of contact all the more remarkable and instructive. The most obvious though not the most important point of resemblance is Barth's development of the Augustinian doctrine of the ontological unreality of evil. Barth himself took pains to differentiate his position on this subject from what he believed to be the Christian Science position, but the same deep concern for the sovereignty and absolute goodness of God runs through them both.

Christian Scientists like most other Christians would find Barth's early emphasis on God as the "wholly other" unduly dualistic, leaving poor humankind shivering in the cold. To be sure, Christian Scientists share his rejection of religious humanism or anthropocentrism. But only with the change signified by his monographs *Evangelical Theology in the 19th Century* and *The Humanity of God* did he move into a position that corresponds in some measure to their own concept of "divinity embracing humanity in Life and its demonstration,—reducing to human perception and understanding the Life which is God."[15] For both theologies, valid thinking must reach down from God's sovereignty rather than up from humanity's limitations.

The analogy cannot be pressed too far. The huge gap that remains is marked by the word *demonstration*. In a brilliant paper on theodicy and the holocaust, Stephen Gottschalk notes that Barth rejects Christian Science "in the very section of the *Church Dogmatics* in which he most clearly identifies sickness and pain as forms of nothingness *[das Nichtige]*." Barth also acknowledged, Gottschalk points out, that "Western Christianity, especially Protestantism, had 'too long succeeded in minimizing and devaluating' the healing ministry of the Gospel."[16] However, as with Tillich, who put great emphasis on spiritual healing in his writings, Barth's observation remained theoretical.

An appreciative review of Barth's *Evangelical Theology: An Introduction* in the *Christian Science Monitor* in 1963 by A. W. Phinney (now editor of the denomination's religious periodicals) ended with a caveat that touches on this lack of firsthand provability:

> Barth's limitation of the role of theology to knowing "the Word of God only at second hand, only in the mirror and echo of the Biblical witness," will not do. The human heart cries out for the perspective of Paul as possible, practical and immediate: "But we all, with open face beholding as in a glass the glory of the Lord, are changed into the same image from glory to glory, even as by the Spirit of the Lord."[17]

The heart cries out for God, Spirit, as tangible reality, acting on and in experience here and now. Eddy remarked in a passage quoted earlier that from childhood she had yearned "for something higher and better than matter, and apart from it"—something more concrete and lasting than matter, however. This radical rejection of matter as nothing more than temporal appearance has been the great scandal of Christian Science from the beginning.

"Christ crucified," we are told in 1 Corinthians, was "unto the Jews a stumblingblock, and unto the Greeks foolishness." In the case of Christian Science, its teaching of the ontological unreality of matter was for many years quite evidently the chief obstacle to its being given serious consideration by either Christian traditionalists or scientific skeptics. Many of these might find it easy to regard the great philosophical idealists of the past with at least a modicum of respect. The philosopher's denial of matter's reality could be tolerated as ingenious theory, entitled to its place in the wide spectrum of metaphysical speculation without seriously challenging the natural order of things as they "obviously" are. But to advance the unreality of matter as a proposition with unbelievable practical consequences was a different matter, not helped at all by the fact that the claim was made by a woman with no philosophic credentials and no extensive formal training in theology or physiology.

What exactly did Eddy mean, then, when she spoke of matter as unreal or illusory?

In the first place, consciousness was primary. Matter, she held, was a false mode of consciousness—the way in which the human mind represents to itself symbolically its present sense of reality, substance, and energy. The body, like everything material, was to be recognized as a construct of consciousness. The primacy of the spiritual, as expressed in the phenomenon of Christian healing, was a fact of being rather than a philosophical postulate or a mystical presentiment. For Jesus, who "plunged beneath the material surface of things, and found the spiritual cause,"[18] matter was an impossible limit on spiritual power. Viewed in this perspective, the whole material creation could be categorized as a faulty interpretation of reality, rather than reality itself. The real locus of experience was the mind. That was where the crucial battles must be fought between reality and appearance.

Today the new physics has changed the whole intellectual atmosphere in regard to matter. There has been literally and figuratively a quantum leap in regard to matter's substantiality. Newton's "pebbles on a trackless shore" have been reduced to theoretical quarks in a universe apparently expanding toward ultimate nothingness.

By now Sir James Jeans's 1937 statement that the universe begins to look more like a great thought than a great machine has become a tiresome cliché. The big question for many thinking people is whether the cosmic Mind that could conceivably have thought (or willed) the universe into being has the chilling qualities of a supremely brilliant mathematician-cum-chemist, for whom the human race might well be only an incidental and very minor experiment. Or could that Mind by any chance be the infinitely compassionate mind "that was also in Christ Jesus"?

·3·

Being and Well-Being

In dignity of being we ascend.
—*Wordsworth*, The Excursion

Well-being is a perfectly legitimate goal, if it includes others' well-being as well as one's own. And if it also rises above the bare literalism of its dictionary definition as a state of health, happiness, and prosperity. Left at that level, the term has an unfortunate suggestion of smug middle-class comfort, a faint aroma of "positive thinking." These of course are the very characteristics that social critics often attribute to American Protestantism in general and Christian Science in particular.

But well-being has a very different meaning when raised to the level of human dignity and true (spiritual) being—where health is the expression of holiness (or being whole), where happiness is *seeing* truth, and prosperity is the unworldly gift of a Providence that waits only for the cleansing and uplifting of our pitifully inadequate desires.

Job knew (or learned) a thing or two about that. But only Jesus had the temerity to say, "Fear not, little flock; for it is your Father's good pleasure to give you the kingdom" (Luke 12:32)—a kingdom which, if sought *first* and for its own sake, may also bring with it the "added things" the Savior promised. Among those added things, it can be argued, are what might be called without irreverence the fringe benefits of the kingdom of heaven experienced as a present reality: health restored, daily needs met, a peace increasingly independent of circumstance.

Christian Science nonetheless emphasizes, as the New Testament does, that there is a great price to be paid for this kingdom-consciousness. The symbol chosen by Eddy to identify all church publications was a cross encircled by a crown, but in her own writings there are many more references to the cross than to the crown. The cross is "the central emblem of

23

history." It "binds human society into solemn union." We must resolve to "take up the cross," learn through "cross-bearing," have our "love made perfect through the cross," "kiss the cross," recognize that the sort of healing Jesus did can be accomplished today "only by taking up the cross and following Christ in the daily life."[1] A single paragraph in *Science and Health* illustrates a major theme that runs through the book:

> While we adore Jesus, and the heart overflows with gratitude for what he did for mortals,—treading alone his loving pathway up to the throne of glory, in speechless agony exploring the way for us,—yet Jesus spares us not one individual experience, if we follow his commands faithfully; and all have the cup of sorrowful effort to drink in proportion to their demonstration of his love, till all are redeemed through divine Love.[2]

This is a side of Christian Science ignored almost entirely by its critics—and by some of its adherents. William James, who was neither, made the mistake of lumping Christian Science with New Thought, mind cure, and success-philosophy thinking as a religion for the "once-born" rather than the "twice-born." This amalgam he described as the "religion of healthy-mindedness," appealing to people who had never had to wrestle with despair through the dark night of the soul.[3]

Certainly there are Christian Scientists to whom this bland description applies, but just as certainly it is not the authentic teaching of Christian Science or the actual experience of those who have penetrated further into that teaching. Eddy's own experience in coming to the crucial events that marked her historic "emergence into light"[4] is summed up by a perceptive Roman Catholic historian as "the story of a deeply religious nature wrestling with the great issues of life and death, not as abstract theological questions, but as they emerged from the agonizing experiences of a soul that had gone down into the depths."[5] She herself, when told that some readers of the revised 1886 edition of *Science and Health* were saying that they could now "see the meaning of Christian Science," exclaimed: "O! do they see it? How little they dream of the awfulness of its heights and depths."[6]

Awe, along with humility, is not a virtue that abounds in the positive-thinking, self-help cults to which Sydney Ahlstrom and others have given the generic name "harmonial religion." Christian Science has often been included casually in this category, as not essentially different from such look-alike offshoots as Religious Science, Divine Science, Science of Mind, and Absolute Science. Charles Braden makes the point that only two lasting movements—Unity and the New Thought wing of mental healing—can be traced directly to disaffected Christian Scientists who had actually studied with Eddy.[7] But he fails to note that from the early 1880s the multiplying variety of mental science groups—often ephemeral but always eclectic—almost invariably borrowed their basic vocabulary from *Science and Health* to clothe ideas of a radically different order.

Over the years there has been little serious scholarly examination or even awareness of these fundamental differences. (One welcome exception is Stephen Gottschalk's 1973 book *The Emergence of Christian Science in American Religious Life,* and even more specifically his 1987 article "Christian Science and Harmonial Religion" in the *Encyclopedia of the American Religious Experience* edited by Charles Lippy and Peter Williams.) Yet it would be impossible for Christian Science to draw the distinction it does between true being (spiritual) and well-being (material) if its ideas and ideals were indeed essentially the same as, for instance, those that characterize the New Thought tradition.

The basic once-born orientation of the harmonial groups is reflected in their dropping of the Christian emphasis on the "new birth," on the necessity for putting off the old self and putting on the new, on the concepts of repentance, redemption, and regeneration, on the meaning of Jesus' sacrifice in the crucifixion, on the nature and subtlety of sin. They lack also the crucial distinction that Christian Science draws between the divine Mind and the unregenerate human mind—the mortal or carnal mind described by Paul as "enmity against God." There is not a trace in harmonial literature of the Puritan iron to be found in *Science and Health*—for example, "Sin is the image of the beast, to be effaced by the sweat of agony"[8]—or in Eddy's message to her church in 1901:

> A sinner ought not to be at ease, or he would never quit sinning. The most deplorable sight is to contemplate the infinite blessings that divine Love bestows on mortals, and their ingratitude and hate, filling up the measure of wickedness against all light. I can conceive of little short of the old orthodox hell to waken such a one from his deluded sense; for all sin is a deluded sense, and dis-ease in sin is better than ease. Some mortals may even need to hear the following thunderbolt of Jonathan Edwards . . .[9]

and then follows a ripsnorting passage from his famous—or infamous?—Enfield sermon: "Sinners in the Hands of an Angry God."

Such sentiments as these are not a mere irrelevance or inconsistency in Eddy's metaphysics. As Karl Holl put it with unwitting understatement, there is a "certain connection" to be found between (1) this evangelical emphasis on salvation from the sin inherent in mortal existence and (2) the metaphysical premise that one's true, spiritual being as the sinless child of

God is progressively demonstrable in human experience. As Christian Scientists see it, this "connection" is actually the Christ, the eternal Truth revealed and exemplified in Jesus and in this age comprehensible as science—and demonstrable as healing.

Eddy's writings show that for her the search for truth always took precedence over the concern for healing. The very title *Science and Health* points in that direction, and the space devoted to theology and metaphysics in the book is very much greater than that devoted to the healing of disease. "The time for thinkers has come," the preface announces, and then continues: "Truth, independent of doctrines and time-honored systems, knocks at the portal of humanity. . . . Ignorance of God is no longer the stepping-stone to faith." With similar emphasis the last sentence of the preface dedicates the pages that follow "to honest seekers for Truth." Truth (capitalized) is the one synonym the author used for both God and his Christ—that is, Truth as Supreme Being, the I AM of all that really is, and Truth as the manifest power of God operative in human consciousness.

All this contrasts markedly with the great flood of harmonial and "success" literature from the 1880s to the present day, most of which is plainly aimed at achieving health, wealth, peace of mind, happiness, power, self-confidence, popularity, and so on, by keeping "in tune with the infinite." Writers in that area tend to speak a good deal about the "God within" or the "Christ within," terms far closer to the psychology of Quimby than to the theology of Eddy, and for the most part frankly pantheistic. The somewhat repellent optimism and insistence on the innate goodness of the human personality, as well as the emphasis in that literature on manipulating material circumstances through mental suggestion, willpower, psychic energy, or personal magnetism, put something of a strain even on the genial Jamesian category of once-born healthy-mindedness.

This doesn't mean that there are not sincere Christians who have found encouragement and inspiration in the extensive literature of New Thought and positive thinking. Nor does it mean that there are not Christian Scientists who unfortunately value their own religion for the loaves and fishes rather than for the "hard saying" which followed that recorded miracle in the Gospel of John: "Except ye eat the flesh of the Son of man, and drink his blood, ye have no life in you" (John 6:53). The consecration needed to make the Christ-consciousness the very substance of one's own thinking and to let the currents of the Christ-love flow through one's own living is not, Eddy warned, to be had at a bargain price.

Gottschalk in his book on the development of Christian Science through the period 1885–1910 devotes the last forty-five pages to a realistic assessment of the secularizing tendencies in the Christian Science movement at that time. Eddy and her more serious students were well aware of this danger, which would change the emphasis from seeking the kingdom of God to seeking the fringe benefits. Today also, experienced practitioners often find it necessary to remind patients that Christian Science is not here merely to make them "comfortable in matter."

The Christian Science movement grew up in a business culture, and since its mission embraced the healing of disabilities and difficulties of every kind, this naturally included business and financial problems. It was all too easy to slip from the delighted discovery that one's religion *worked* in this area of experience to seeing it as a means of achieving worldly success. Gottschalk, who rightly points out the pragmatic element in Christian Science—as indeed in New Testament Christianity—goes on to say:

> To the degree that Christian Science was secularized in practice . . . its character as a pragmatic grasp of Christian revelation was vitiated. The point can be stated in terms of two ways in which the term *pragmatic* may be used. In its larger and more philosophic sense, *pragmatic* signifies a quality of being experientially meaningful. But in its lesser and more popular usage, it connotes convenience and mere expediency. The secularized practice of Christian Science amounts to the reduction of a pragmatic religious teaching in the larger sense to a pragmatic problem-solver in the lesser sense. The teachings that inspire any movement that gains some widespread popularity are, of course, subject to being distorted in practice. But the particular *character* of this distortion in the case of Christian Science can only be understood as an inversion of its basic strength.[10]

It was this debasing of her teachings that Eddy deplored in the constant borrowings from her writings made by "harmonial" writers of all sorts. A useful and thoroughly typical example is a sentence lifted from *Science and Health* and refashioned slightly in a New Thought pamphlet "All Things Are Yours" by one Charles Townsend.[11] Italics are added to emphasize a significant change in meaning introduced by the borrower:

> Prayer cannot change the unalterable Truth, nor can prayer alone give us an understanding of Truth; but prayer, coupled with a fervent habitual desire to know and do the will of God, *will bring us into all Truth*. (Eddy)

> Truth cannot be changed by prayer; but prayer, which is a real desire to know and do the whole will of God, *will always bring the desired result*. (Townsend)

Unfortunately, such camouflaged reversal of Eddy's teachings has not been limited to defectors from or rivals of the organized movement, as many sincere Christian Scientists are aware. One of the early defectors was cynical enough to prophesy, "When the founder of Christian Science is taken away, its Christianity will disappear with her."[12] Fortunately, that has not happened, but if it did Christian Science itself would obviously disappear—a *Hamlet* without the Prince, a Gospel without a God.

Christianity has taken many forms through the centuries. In regard to this world's goods and the infinite good that is God, it has ranged from the medieval ideal of holy poverty to the nineteenth-century espousal of the gospel of wealth. In the same way, Christians' attitudes toward God have ranged from mortification of the flesh to glorification of the flesh. Christian Science thinking does not fit into either of those extremes, but individual Christian Scientists of varying religious and social backgrounds sometimes show unredeemed inclinations in one direction or the other.

During the 1920s, as Christian Science neared its fiftieth year of institutional existence and American materialism roared along with self-confident abandon toward the Wall Street crash of 1929, two very different social and philosophic observers of the scene made comments on Christian Science which may serve a useful purpose in this discussion.

First is a paragraph from George Santayana's *Character and Opinion in the United States*:

> To be poor in order to be simple, to produce less in order that the product may be more choice and beautiful, and may leave us less burdened with unnecessary duties and useless possessions—that is an ideal not articulate in the American mind; yet here and there I seem to have heard a sigh after it, a groan at the perpetual incubus of business and shrill society. Significant witness to such aspirations is borne by those new forms of popular religion, not mere variations on tradition, which have sprung up from the soil—revivalism, spiritualism, Christian Science, the New Thought. Whether or not we can tap, through these or other channels, some cosmic or other energy not hitherto at the disposal of man (and there is nothing incredible in that), we certainly may try to remove friction and waste in the mere process of living; we may relax morbid strains, lessen suppressed instincts, iron out the creases of the soul, discipline ourselves into simplicity, sweetness, and peace. These religious movements are efforts toward such physiological economy and hygiene; and while they are thoroughly plebeian, with no great lights, and no idea of raising men from the most vulgar and humdrum worldly existence, yet they see the possibility of physical and moral health on that common plane, and pursue it. That is true morality.[13]

The negatives toward the end of this statement are undeserved so far as genuine Christian Science is concerned, whether or not they apply to the miscellaneous bedfellows named along with it. But the charitable insight is suggestive on whatever level. There is certainly a sense in which Christian Science may be viewed as a spiritual hygiene, and although it is by no means confined to the possibility of physical and moral health on the "common plane," that is certainly one of its important functions. On the other hand, to say that it has "no idea of raising men from the most vulgar and humdrum worldly existence" is as far from the facts as could be.

The literature of Christian Science gives evidence of a surprising variety of ways in which human lives have been enriched by what can only be called a spiritual revolution. In many cases this has begun with a bodily healing, but it seldom stops there. Sometimes this healing may be accompanied by a flood of light and joy not unlike the conversion experiences recorded in evangelical literature. A short quotation from a testimonial included in the final chapter, "Fruitage," in *Science and Health* will serve to illustrate this. The testifier after years of family tragedies and illness had been given a copy of the book and had devoured it eagerly. At first she kept "looking back" to see whether she was really free of the "error" that had held her, until one day when she realized

> that to catch a glimpse of what spiritual sense means I must put corporeal sense behind me. I then set to work in earnest to find the true way. I opened *Science and Health* and these words were before me, "If God were understood, instead of being merely believed, this understanding would establish health" (p. 203). I saw that I must get the right understanding of God! I closed the book and with head bowed in prayer I waited with longing intensity for some answer. How long I waited I do not know, but suddenly, like a wonderful burst of sunlight after a storm, came clearly this thought, "Be still, and know that I am God." I held my breath—deep into my hungering thought sank the infinite meaning of that "I." All self-conceit, egotism, selfishness, everything that constitutes the mortal "I," sank abashed out of sight. I trod, as it were, on holy ground. Words are inadequate to convey the fulness of that spiritual uplifting, but others who have had similar experiences will understand.[14]

Such an experience is like a rock thrown into a pond. If it is more than a pebble or a transitory emotion, it will send out a series of concentric ripples that may finally extend to the entire shoreline of the pond. The new spiritual concept of self and body involved in the experience can gradually reach the whole body of complex concepts and relationships that appear to condition one's living.

Christian Science again has links with the evangelical tradition in its emphasis on individual salvation. But unlike the self-help cults with which it is so often confused, its ultimate aim is world salvation. An official 1966 publication of the church comments somewhat realistically on this point in relation to the social implications of being "born again." It starts by quoting Eddy's statement: "The new birth is not the work of a moment. It begins with moments, and goes on with years; moments of surrender to God, of childlike trust and joyful adoption of good; moments of self-abnegation, self-con-secration, heaven-born hope, and spiritual love."[15] Then it continues:

> This new sense of being cannot help but overflow in active love for others—first, perhaps, in one's more immediate relationships, eventually in new awarenesses, insights, and outreachings to society at large. Sooner or later it must result in shaking up those entrenched personal predilec-tions which breed intolerance and are so often mistaken for eternal truths. When Spirit is accepted as the only absolute, the relativity of all human positions becomes gradually evident. . . .
>
> Whether a Christian Scientist participates in the social battles of our day as a liberal or a conservative, a fighter or a reconciler, a partisan or an independent, a private or a general, his ultimate purpose is to *heal*. Yet most Christian Scientists would probably agree that up to now only a small fraction of the healing dynamic of their religion has been utilized in relation to the urgent collective problems facing the world.[16]

This leads us back to a second 1920s judgment by a European observer of the American scene, more controversial than Santayana's comment but in some ways more discriminating. It occurs in a book by the then much quoted social philosopher Count Hermann Keyserling. In his *America Set Free*, published in the very year of the stock-market disaster that so dramatically shook America's runaway optimism, he wrote:

> *If* matter is overemphasized in the United States, and *if* there is such a thing as spiritual reality, then it follows *a priori*, from the general knowl-edge we have of the human soul, that spirituality in America should differentiate with equal onesidedness. So it actually does; the quality of "purity" determined by Puritanism, in its turn, adds to the clearness of the contours. Further: *if* the fundamental attitude in the United States is one of spiritual passivity, then some attitude which is all the more pronounced in its activity must needs compensate it in the general system. This is precisely the meaning of the uncompromising affirmations and denials of Christian Science. . . . We thus find that every spiritual American who can be considered as representative, actually belongs, whether he knows it or not, to the wider circle of Christian Science. It would perhaps be more correct, from the point of view of fact, to say that somehow or other he

belongs to New Thought. Emerson, for instance, undoubtedly did, whereas one could not have called him a Christian Scientist. But on the plane of significance, Christian Science and no other expression of American religiousness stands out as the prototype.[17]

Keyserling recognized the possible objection that what he called the "primitivity of the notions of Christian Science" made these "notions" unfit to "express truth in any way." But he proceeded to reject this argument with an ingenious comparison between American and Russian spirituality. Europe, he wrote, often regards with awe the vast capacity for suffering and the passionate eschatology of primitive Russian religiosity, but the active, healing, transforming character of the new American religion should be recognized as being just as representative of "pure spirituality." Both, he emphasized, are far removed "from a normal European religion"—just as far, perhaps, as a normal European religion is from primitive Christianity!

As sociology, these generalizations seem to come from an age of innocence remote from our present era of reliance on computerized "hard" facts for our social theories—a development of scientific materialism anatomized with admirable insight and precision in William Barrett's aptly named *Death of the Soul*.[18]

Any just estimate of Christian Science today must put it into that larger context; it cannot be adequately explained or understood as merely a late nineteenth-century American cultural phenomenon. It must also be weighed against the secular values and the scientific achievements of the late twentieth century and the whole flow of Western thought since the Enlightenment.

It will be the function of the second half of this book to examine what contributions, if any, Christian Science has made or may make to the extraordinary world we live in today. But for that we must take one more look at how its founder's original vision has held up so far. She herself saw clearly the danger of substituting "the great bitch-goddess Success" for the divine Father-Mother from whom all excellence proceeds. Can the movement she founded maintain—and demonstrate—the crucial distinction she drew between well-being as spiritual grace and well-being as earthly goal?

·4·

Sexuality and Spirituality

So God created man in his own image . . .
male and female created he them.
—*Genesis 1:27*

Mary Baker Eddy was by no means the first religious leader to recognize God as Mother as well as Father. But she was the first to give this concept the distinctive metaphysical significance it has in Christian Science.

From the Old Testament prophets to the New England Transcendentalists of the nineteenth century, there had been religious men and women who bore witness to their vivid glimpses of God's feminine as well as masculine nature. For years Theodore Parker prayed publicly each Sunday morning in Boston: "Our Father and our Mother God," and the last of the Transcendentalists, Cyrus Bartol, in 1873 wrote wistfully of "the heavenly Mother as well as Father" whom we need.[1]

Whatever they—and earlier visionaries like Jacob Boehme, Emanuel Swedenborg, and Mother Ann Lee—meant by such expressions, their words suggested to many people an actual dualism in God. The same casual assumption has been made in regard to Eddy's use of the term Father-Mother, and it has often been mistakenly described as belief in a bisexual or androgynous God.

The fact is that the very concept of sex is outside the Christian Science understanding of Deity. Sex belongs wholly to the finite human sense of being, with its endless dualisms of night and day, cold and hot, up and down, mind and matter, life and death. Even if one sees any of these pairs as indicating a continuum rather than a rigid polarity, they remain outside the undivided oneness of God—mere benchmarks of finitude.

This is not to deny that the divine Mind expresses itself in infinite variety throughout its universe of spiritual "ideas." But (Christian Science would

33

add) not through the limiting categories imposed by our physical senses and our imperfect apprehension of spiritual reality. This view carries to a logical conclusion Paul's radical assertion that there is "no such thing as Jew and Greek, slave and freeman, male and female; for you are all one person in Christ Jesus."[2]

Ultimately, Christian Science holds, each individual finds his or her unique spiritual identity not as a male or a female, a Frenchman or a Zulu, but as a deeply loved and wonderfully original "child" of the universal Father-Mother. To catch even a glimpse of this new yet always existent selfhood is to begin the process of new birth and the gradual freeing of one's experience from the tyranny of material circumstance and happenstance. At the same time this process necessarily involves a widening, more all-embracing concept of "spiritual man," defined by *Science and Health* in part as "the compound idea of God, including all right ideas; the generic term for all that reflects God's image and likeness."[3]

And here we run into a semantic difficulty peculiar to our times. There is no way of explaining Christian Science theology without using the word *man* occasionally in its traditional generic sense, wholly nonsexist in its intent. Used in that way, it has in Christian Science a special metaphysical meaning that differentiates it completely from all the generic terms like humanity, humankind, people, persons, mortals, and so on, which most of us now try to substitute for *man* in a frantic effort to avoid sexist language. But man as spiritual idea is something entirely different from—although crucially important to—the sinning race of mortals, of men and women evolved from primeval slime.

Thus, in choosing to describe God as Father and/or Mother, one is using the words metaphorically. While they suggest the uniting of two complementary sets of characteristics and functions, they are not meant to suggest a method of procreation and a consequent physical man-woman-child relationship that are far from reflecting the perfect unity of God and spiritual man.

In a brief 1885 address to two thousand disapproving Evangelicals in Boston's Tremont Temple, Eddy explained that not knowing "what the person of omnipotence and omnipresence is, or what the infinite includes," she worshipped "that of which I can conceive, first, as a loving Father and Mother." Then, she added, "as thought ascends the scale of being to diviner consciousness" God became to her what he was to the apostle who declared "God is love"—the divine Principle of being.[4] In coupling Principle and Love, as she frequently did, one might say that she was marrying the masculine concept of law to the feminine concept of grace—or better, seeing them as already one. In doing this she was essentially anticipating those contemporary theologians, including Boston's Mary Daly, who argue that God must be recognized as verb as well as noun, process as well as substance.

There is a further dimension to this subject that is seldom spelled out explicitly but has an important bearing on Christian Science theology. Throughout the Christian era there has been a tendency to regard human beings as the joint product of a Heavenly Father and an Earth Mother. God the Father provided the soul, Mother Nature the body. The image of God was to be found in the mind of mortals, the instincts of nature (or in Pauline terms the natural man) in a material body. The very etymological connection between *mater* and such words as *material, matrix, matter* points to woman the child-bearer as the passive recipient, instrument, and sometimes spoiler of the godlike evolutionary purpose of the superior male intelligence.

This, of course, is a very rough simplification of much more sophisticated philosophic and metaphysical theories, but it does indicate a deep-lying though often unconscious assumption in much human thinking. And it is directly challenged by the Christian Science conviction that if God, Spirit, is the sole source of our true being, then as "children" of that all-powerful, all-encompassing Father-Mother we must in reality be wholly and purely spiritual.

MORES AND MORALS

What is the *practical* effect of that conviction on a human consciousness to which matter still seems very real and the physiological, psychological, and social aspects of sexuality present immense and complex challenges?

First of all, it provides a firm spiritual base for equality of the sexes in human affairs. It does not ask for women half the world as men have made it; it asks, for both women and men, the world as God has made it—the "kingdom" Christ offers as present fact, not merely future promise.

To the extent that this is apprehended, sexist stereotypes may be transcended in practice and a mutual enrichment of the two sexes follows, with a greater sharing of roles and values traditionally assigned to one sex or the other. This, of course, has already been taking place in society on a large scale, closely allied with the concurrent revolution of sexual mores and bringing with it a flock of new psychological, social, and economic problems. Christian Scientists tend to welcome what they would call the "higher" aspects of this change. But there is an immense distance between the sexual revolution's discarding of traditional Christian morality and the radical spiritual emphasis of Christian Science that would provide fresh underpinnings for the original Christian ideal of keeping sexual activity within the marriage relationship.

The metaphysical basis for this approach may be illustrated by three short passages from *Science and Health:*

> Union of the masculine and feminine qualities constitutes completeness. The masculine mind reaches a higher tone through certain elements of the feminine, while the feminine mind gains courage and strength through masculine qualities. These different elements conjoin naturally with each other, and their true harmony is in spiritual oneness. . . .

> In Science man is the offspring of Spirit. The beautiful, good, and pure constitute his ancestry. His origin is not, like that of mortals, in brute instinct, nor does he pass through material conditions prior to reaching intelligence. Spirit is his primitive and ultimate source of being; God is his Father, and Life is the law of his being. . . .

> Emerge gently from matter into Spirit. Think not to thwart the spiritual ultimate of all things, but come naturally into Spirit through better health and morals and as the result of spiritual growth.[5]

Today the word *morals* has an antiquated sound, even while *spiritual* enjoys a notable renascence. Christian Science holds that while morality is something less than spirituality, the two are far from unrelated. There is a distinction, however, between genuine Christian morality and the harsh moralism that has often claimed its name. To oversimplify a little, it is the difference between Old Testament judgment and New Testament healing. In defending what has seemed to some people an excessively conservative position on sexual morality, the Church of Christ, Scientist, has often pointed to the incident in John 8 wherein Jesus meets the woman taken in adultery. Jesus—as always, compassionate and, as always, realistic—deftly lifted the savage Mosaic penalty but *healed* the sinner. For adultery, to him, was obviously a sin, not a casual happening to be shrugged off lightly as in our permissive age. So with the power of healing forgiveness he could say to the accused woman, "Neither do I condemn thee: go and *sin no more.*" Here, Christian Science would say, moral judgment is the servant of spiritual redemption.

To give this a larger application, I am taking the liberty of adapting the words of an official reply to a church member who had written to the Boston headquarters protesting the Church's position that homosexuality is a matter for healing rather than for automatic endorsement as a perfectly natural and satisfactory life-style. The member's complaint showed that she considered sexual orientation to be a fixed fact that determines a human being's identity once and forever. This, the reply pointed out, would make anyone's sexual proclivities more important than his or her spiritual identity. Such an assumption would leave out of account the fact that many people, both homosexual and heterosexual, have been lifted by Christian Science out of all sorts of morally questionable situations, propensities, and practices. These have usually seemed "natural" to them until they came to understand the purity and freedom of their true spiritual identities. Paul, the letter reminded the complainant, writes that "the natural man receiveth not the things of the Spirit of God: for they are foolishness unto him: neither can he know them, because they are spiritually discerned."

Surely, the letter went on, no one can have anything but compassion for a young Christian Scientist who is spiritually alert enough to know that he or she *can* be healed of a strong homosexual orientation and is struggling to make that demonstration. The same thing, it added, would be true of a husband or wife desperately trying to save a marriage threatened by an extramarital affair, or an unmarried man driven by seemingly irresistible impulses to a constant resort to prostitutes, or a young woman physically unattractive who despairingly longs for marriage and sees no prospect of ever achieving it. Christian Science doesn't promise them a busy sexual life, either within or without the traditional Christian standards of morality. But it does offer each one a life purified and enriched by an increasing recognition of his or her true spiritual being, with more and more freedom from the bondage of obsessive sensuality.

We live in an age that frequently seems to make sexual activity the central fact of existence. It is often prized not merely as the procreative mechanism responsible for human existence but also as the supreme recreational privilege granted to humanity. As such, some hold, it is to be freely indulged, unhampered by traditional Christian ideals and moral taboos. Even conservative Christian churches are reconsidering long-held views on masturbation, homosexuality, and premarital sex. In this respect Eddy was closer to the Pauline standard of morality than to the more relaxed standards of present-day liberal Protestantism, and on the whole that holds true for her followers today. As a spokesperson for the Church of Christ, Scientist, remarked laconically in a 1982 newspaper interview, "The Church can't change every time a social trend changes."[6]

Eddy took the position that so long as mortals conceived themselves to be physical organisms, sexual activity (within the marriage relationship) would be necessary for the propagation of the race, but that sensuality for its own sake would be progressively outgrown as thought became more spiritualized.

"Higher enjoyments alone can satisfy the cravings of immortal man," she wrote. "The good in human affections must have ascendency over the evil and the spiritual over the animal, or happiness will never be won."[7]

Austere as such statements may sound to the contemporary ear, they are tempered by her admonition to emerge "gently" from matter into Spirit. At its worst, a marriage may be no more than "legalized lust,"[8] but at its best it can be "a union of the affections that tends to lift mortals higher."[9] Ideally it should lead away from mere self-gratification to the enriching (if exacting) challenges of family life.

Most Christian Scientists accept family planning as normal, although abortions are rare because of medical as well as moral considerations. A good deal of emphasis is put on the healing of marital difficulties and discordant family conditions, although the record of avoiding divorce is not notably better than that in other Protestant denominations. Occasional teenage pregnancies and youthful rebellions of all sorts occur in Christian Science families much as in other church-going, middle-class households. When a Christian Science practitioner is appealed to for help in regard to such problems, the practitioner's work is not to give human counseling. It is, rather, to open the thought of those concerned to the healing presence and guidance of the divine Mind in even the most complex situations.

The Church makes few dogmatic pronouncements on specific sexual problems. Nor does it need to, since all these problems are seen within the metaphysical and scriptural framework epitomized in Jesus' words: "It is the spirit that quickeneth; the flesh profiteth nothing" (John 6:63). To take a single example, a Christian Scientist addicted to the practice of masturbation and to the unbridled fantasizing that so often accompanies it would certainly feel the need for the spiritual growth that would free him or her from this unwanted compulsion. In other words, it would call for healing rather than either self-condemnation or resigned acceptance. The same thing would be true of gluttony or any other addictive habit that made one the prisoner rather than the master of fleshly appetites. The challenge is not merely moral; basically it is metaphysical, as the next section of this chapter makes clear.

As to sexual liaisons outside marriage, it is unlikely that anyone in such a situation would be elected to office in a Christian Science church, nor would he or she be eligible for listing as a practitioner in the *Christian Science Journal* until a full healing of the situation had taken place. The same thing is true of anyone leading an active homosexual life. In the United States several small groups calling themselves Christian Science Gays and Lesbians militantly maintain that there is no need for their being "healed" of their orientation—that, in fact, such healing is neither desirable nor possible. These groups ardently resist the evidence of homosexuality healed by Christian Science and lives given a more fulfilling direction. However, the aim in all such healing is not merely sexual reorientation; it is, rather, the Christian ideal of spiritual regeneration, described by Eddy as "making mankind better physically, morally, and spiritually."

In recent years the weekly and monthly testimonials published in Christian Science periodicals have included an increasing number of healings of family and personal problems connected with sex. Occasionally the name of a testifier may be withheld because of the intimate nature of the facts revealed. A pattern that occurs from time to time, with variations, is found in accounts by individuals who were brought up in a Christian Science family but drifted away to the allurements of the pot party and the singles bar, only to turn back to Christian Science for help at a much later period of disillusionment or urgent need. It is not uncommon then for them to find that what had once seemed pious abstractions were now coming to the rescue as powerful, liberating, operative truths. These stories have their analogues in the experiences of repentant prodigals of other faiths, but they are without the melodramatic tone frequently found in accounts by the hot gospelers of yesterday and the electronic evangelists of today.

FEMINISM AND CHAUVINISM

The feminist note so often struck in the more sophisticated religious literature of our age is also to be found in the Christian Science periodicals, but with less of a crusading ring to it than is common in such writing. This is understandable, since Eddy's followers have stood quietly but practically for equality of the sexes for more than a hundred years. Ironically, men still predominate in the top ranks of the "mother" church organization, but women are to be found in important executive positions at all levels and greatly predominate in the crucial roles of Christian Science practitioners and teachers. Although there are still skirmishes to be fought over the remaining traces of male domination in the organization, the far greater task is to demonstrate an effective balance of feminine and masculine *qualities* in the living of Christian Science. And essential to this task is a deeper understanding of the oneness of these qualities in the divine Father-Mother who, to the Christian Scientist, is both Principle and Love. In this particular, one finds a certain parallelism between Eddy's theology and Simone Weil's.

Oddly enough, there has been no greater misunderstanding of this basic theological point than is evidenced in the writings of feminist scholars in the field of religion. By now, twentieth-century feminism has developed its own conflicting extremes and disparities, yet with almost unbroken unanimity feminist writers on religion have chosen to describe Christian Science and its founder in the loaded stereotypical terms used by enraged nineteenth-century males against "public" women encroaching on sacrosanct masculine territory.

I remember showing to a Christian Scientist friend some years ago just such an article by a woman anthropologist whom we both knew personally. My friend read the article, with its description of Eddy as "a classic female hysteric" who used Christian Science as a means to achieve "an extraordinary power role" and attracted to her movement frustrated women eager to satisfy their craving for "dominance" in a male society. My friend's laconic comment on the author's interpretation: "She's a male chauvinist!"

As a biographer of Eddy and student of Christian Science history, I have been fascinated to see feminist writers through several decades accepting without question the chauvinistic interpretations of such early male writers on this subject as Mark Twain, Pierre Janet, Stefan Zweig, E. F. Dakin, and H. L. Mencken. The stock explanation of Eddy's founding of the Christian Science movement, repeated *ad nauseam*, is "her naked urge to dominate," to gain "power, status, and prestige," through "a series of destructive power struggles between herself and men and women whom she perceived as threatening her singular domination."[10]

Statements of this kind, drawn almost entirely from polemic sources, accompanied occasionally by a few scraps of heavily misinterpreted "documentation," ignore completely the serious scholarship of the past twenty years on this subject. When it comes to presenting Eddy's theology, some of these accounts drop to an almost comic-strip level of distortion. Even some highly respected and ordinarily responsible feminist scholars have fallen into this trap, illustrating the strength of a tradition unconsciously adopted from a long line of *parti pris* male critics of Christian Science.

An astonishing example of this occurs in the first volume of *Women and Religion in America* by Rosemary Radford Ruether and Rosemary Skinner Keller. Eddy, the book states flatly, "regarded the Feminine as the principle of spiritual perfection" and "identified maleness with carnality and materialism." This is an interesting fantasy but, it so happens, completely contrary to Eddy's published views. The same is true of Ruether's later hypostatizing of two supposed "principles" of Christian Science: a "Masculine Principle of material force" and a "Feminine Principle as superior to the coarse, materialist Masculine Principle."[11]

This concept of an "androgynous" god composed of two opposing principles, good and bad, looks like something taken from Zoroastrianism. It certainly has nothing to do with Eddy's theology, which constantly emphasizes that God is the one and only Principle of all that really is. From this follows the deduction that one's true spiritual identity as the expression or reflection of the one infinite, undivided Principle necessarily embraces all the spiritual qualities that human beings may think of as masculine or feminine. This is the metaphysical position that underlies the ethical commitment of Christian Science to the equality of the sexes.

In several places Eddy realistically indicates that the "feminine" quality of love may convey to human sense the clearest idea of God, but Love understood as the very Principle of all true being has no sexist association whatever. On the more relative level she wrote: "The ideal man corresponds to creation, to intelligence, and to Truth. The ideal woman corresponds to Life and to Love." At the same time, she looked forward to the day when "white-robed purity will unite in one person masculine wisdom and feminine love, spiritual understanding and perpetual peace."[12]

I have confined myself to a single example of the strange lapse in feminist scholarship in dealing with Eddy and Christian Science—a lapse in elementary factual accuracy, let alone in responsible interpretation. This all too familiar phenomenon was at last very ably dissected in a 1986 article by Jean McDonald in the *Journal of Feminist Studies in Religion*.[13] Its persuasive thesis was that the stereotyped portrait of Mary Baker Eddy in the feminist literature of this century "matches in striking detail the traditional male portrait of 'public' women who have left their 'proper sphere,' thus potentially threatening men." The article's meticulous and wide-ranging documentation from largely ignored primary sources entitles its author to make a further useful criticism:

> The tendency of traditional male historians to rely predominantly on secondary sources for their studies of women's lives—a casual approach men have not pursued when studying men—means that we are unlikely to find the reasons for women's behavior. Surprisingly, feminist scholarship on Eddy is also based largely on secondary sources rather than on original sources that allow women to interpret their own experience. Turning to the original evidence will give us not only better scholarship but better *feminist* scholarship.

More important than that, however, is the fact that Christian Science is misconceived if it is seen merely as a woman's movement. The evidence is overwhelming that the most common reasons why men and women alike have turned to it are (1) for healing, and (2) for a better, more satisfying understanding of God and the Bible. The search for a believable theodicy is not confined to either sex. Although the word *theodicy* is not one that most people know, millions hunger for the *what, how, why,* and *if* of a God they can rationally trust, whose justice and care they can *prove* to themselves in their daily experience.

There is no inherent reason why scholarship by either sex should ignore such simple motivations and their possible relationship to primitive Christianity. A particularly useful illustration of this can be found by turning back once again to that age of demi-innocence, the late 1920s. Mary Burt Messer, an early feminist and sociologist who later became a Christian Science practitioner, included in a chapter entitled "The Advance of Woman" in her 1928 book *The Family in the Making* a few pages on what she called "a conception of the Christian religion drawn from woman's insight, quietly advancing woman to a position of equality with man in the Christian church, and conceiving the spiritual or creative principle in feminine as well as in masculine terms."[14] Here in Christian Science, she added, was "something which has actually proceeded from a differentiated value in womankind—not discoverable in woman as a unique possession, but conserved in her or revealed through her as a further reach of the perceptive possibilities of the human race."

But this value Messer also saw as recapturing a "primitive Christian meaning, once registered by illuminated men and thereafter lost"—the meaning and possibility of Christian healing. Christian Science, she concluded, revived "the early Christian emphasis on the inner or spiritual man, as distinguished from the material personality, the man of flesh, but the relation between the divine and human at this point is wrought out in a way which departs widely from the asceticism of the Middle Ages in that it provides for the ascent of man through the upward steps of a natural life."

Messer went so far as to ask whether this spiritual development might not be seen eventually as "a contribution to the larger 'science' that must avail itself of every true perception and attribute of mind in its quest for knowledge." And as though that question were not bold enough, her final words on the subject could be counted upon to upset those for whom all value judgments must give place to quantitative measurement and statistical analysis:

> Interestingly enough this unique feminine contribution may be broadly classified as falling in the field of deductive thought and in this sense fulfilling to a degree at least the prophecy of [the British historian] Buckle, who believed that the cultural gift of woman was not to be identified wholly

with that of man, but was to be advanced as a distinct addition to or amplification of his powers of thought. It may be said further of this feminine gift that it verifies a certain profound wisdom in the world's platitudes in that it confirms the age-old association of woman with the ministry of love.

To all of which one might append as a contrasting touch of 1980s cynicism the statement that John Updike puts into the mouth of the raunchy protagonist of *Roger's Version:* "Christian Science! as if there could be such a thing!"[15]

·5·

Science and Health

to gyve science & helthe to his puple. . . .
—Luke 1:77 (Wyclif)

SCIENCE

With the extraordinary developments in biophysics, biochemistry, and biomedicine in this century, the age-old art of healing can now lay claim to being a science—the youngest science, as Dr. Lewis Thomas calls it.

Yet science itself is today hedged about with caveats. First came the quantum physicists, with their uncertainty and complementarity principles, their neurons and neutrinos and antiparticles and probability waves. All of which point to such prognoses as Wolfgang Pauli's 1952 pronouncement:

> Since the discovery of the elementary quantum, physics was obliged to renounce its proud claim to be able to understand in principle the *whole* of the world. But this predicament may contain the seed of further developments which will correct the previous one-sided orientation and will move towards a unitary world-view in which science is only a part in the whole.[1]

As medical biology in the mid-century leaped forward with exhilarated self-confidence, René Dubos sounded an early warning: "Exact sciences give correct answers to certain aspects of life problems, but very incomplete answers."[2] And in the present decade President Derek Bok of Harvard, in an impressive report on the current status and needs of the university's medical school, remarks almost casually:

> Fewer doctors are now inclined to think of themselves as simply arriving at logically determined conclusions by applying scientifically tested truths to experimentally derived data. . . . In short, the doctor's world cannot be restricted to science or neatly divided between the known and the un-

45

known. Considerations of many kinds are often jumbled together to form a picture full of uncertainties, requiring the most delicate kinds of judgments and intuitions.[3]

Those considerations are (among other things) economic, political, social, legal, psychological, technological, institutional, ethical, cultural, philosophic, philanthropic, theological, spiritual.

A growing recognition of this complexity (or to use an expression from *Science and Health,* these "interlaced ambiguities") has to some degree opened the way for a more widespread consideration of healing methods other than those certified by the organized medical industry. The alternative options include, of course, spiritual healing. Today we may be a little closer to the realization of Mary Burt Messer's 1928 conjecture that eventually even Christian Science would be seen as "a contribution to the larger 'science' that must avail itself of every true perception and attribute of mind in its quest for knowledge."[4]

The most palpable indication of this is the rather astonishing revival of spiritual healing in the mainstream Christian churches in the past half century. More than ninety years ago Eddy made a prediction even more controversial than Messer's. "If the lives of Christian Scientists attest their fidelity to Truth," she wrote, "I predict that in the twentieth century every Christian church in our land, and a few in far-off lands, will approximate the understanding of Christian Science sufficiently to heal the sick in his name."[5] The sentence contained two important—but frequently overlooked—qualifying words: the initial *If* and the verb *approximate.*

In the spectrum of Christian healing there are widely varying degrees of "approximate" understanding between Christian Scientists who rely wholly on prayer for healing and Christian healers who see prayer as a support to medical treatment rather than a substitute for it. At one extreme are some Christian Scientists who would dismiss all other forms of spiritual healing as "mere" faith cures; at the other extreme are some spiritual healers who would write off Christian Science as outside the pale of Christianity and rationality. Fortunately many others in both camps recognize the significant concerns they share, and some who are not Christian Scientists freely acknowledge the important role Christian Science has played in the modern revival of Christian healing.

A useful example of mutual exploration is a 1986 interview in the *Christian Science Sentinel* with a Methodist minister who has been actively committed to spiritual healing for many years. Two brief quotations give the flavor of the recorded dialogue; the italicized portions are the Christian Science interviewer's words:

I think this differing approach to the actual practice of healing is important, however much we share. You place the emphasis on intercessory prayer and symbolic acts such as laying on of hands. Christian Scientists see healing as a matter of the conscientious, heartfelt practice of spiritual law, which they feel Mrs. Eddy conclusively discovered and stated. Is that a fair way to put it?

I think it's a very fair way; yet these acts that you mention here are for me a way of reconciling, coming home again, really. They are ways that symbolically help us come back home and be reconciled with God.

John Wesley spoke very much along the lines of what he called rules for health. They're really something like spiritual laws, including the maintenance of a right kind of attitude and looking at things from the highest and best point of view. I realize this is quite different in some regards from Mrs. Eddy's understanding of spiritual law, since Wesley did believe in the use of certain herbs and foods and medicines. But I think it's important that both saw a connection between health and Christian living.

I agree in basic principle that there are spiritual laws. If we abide by them, we will find ourselves in harmony with the divine plan. It's important to find our way into this plan and to abide by these spiritual principles that God provides for us. But I would be hesitant as to how much we know about them. Perhaps that's why we sometimes fail, because sometimes we don't know them all. . . .

I think we feel, too, it's supremely important to Christianity that this healing be practiced today. What would you say to a Christian Scientist who may be struggling to practice spiritual healing in a pretty adverse mental climate, in which secularism and materialism so often deny that such healing is real?

I would try to encourage that person. I would point to that person and say, "You have hold of a real truth. I think you ought to read the New Testament and read Mrs. Eddy's book *Science and Health* again. Don't give up; hold on to these things." That's what I would say.[6]

Virtually all Christian healers find their spiritual mandate in the New Testament record of the words and works of Jesus and the apostles. This implies a shared conviction that God is a loving Father who wills health of mind and body and soul for his children, who in turn are to be recognized as far more than biochemical organisms or programmed mechanisms. To some spiritual healers, however, outstanding cures are taken as evidence of God's miraculous intervention in human affairs, a feat that would require his arbitrary setting aside of currently accepted laws of nature. To others, such cures are evidence of the operation of higher spiritual laws which show even the marvelous mathematical order of the universe—as conceived by human science—to be only our temporary, imperfect sense of the universe as it exists in the infinite Mind that is God.

To the really serious Christian Scientist the chief function of his or her religion is not merely to make sick people well. Its primary purpose is to bear witness to the true nature of God and his creation. But the witness through healing is essential as concrete evidence of the "superiority of spiritual power over material resistance."[7] In a sense, it may be taken as an extension of the much-disputed statement in the Epistle of James: "Show me thy faith without thy works, and I will show thee my faith by my works."

A witness provides evidence. So where is the evidence of Christian Science healing? Do the "lives of Christian Scientists" which Eddy expected to "attest their fidelity to Truth" provide convincing evidence of the validity of their healing claims? What is to be made of the tens of thousands of letters of testimony published in the Christian Science periodicals during the past hundred years?

As Chapter 9 points out in more detail, these published accounts cannot be considered scientific evidence in the usual sense. They are chunks of experience witnessing to transformed lives as well as to particular healings— accounts voluntarily submitted by real people known in their communities, people vouched for by friends or community members and available to answer questions by seriously interested inquirers.

In 1966 the Church of Christ, Scientist, published a centennial volume— *A Century of Christian Science Healing*—composed largely of representative accounts of healing selected from its own religious periodicals during the preceding hundred years. It was, the foreword announced, "not a study in medicine or in church history but in human lives grasped by the Christ." The emphasis is typical. Vitally important as the humanitarian purpose of healing sickness and suffering is, the "higher mission of the Christ-power" now as in Jesus' time is "to take away the sins of the world."[8] Yet even so, physical healing offers an especially conspicuous sign of the presence and operation of this power. As the centennial volume puts it:

> The healing of physical disease is one of the most concrete proofs that can be offered of the substantiality of Spirit. It is not of itself conclusive, and in the nature of things it cannot be offered under the conditions of controlled experiment. But in conjunction with all the other evidences of spiritual power furnished by Christianity understood as Science it offers a substantial challenge to materialistic assumptions.[9]

A determined skeptic is not likely to be convinced by any particular healing attributed solely to prayer. He or she may dismiss it on hypothetical grounds of coincidence, a misdiagnosis, spontaneous remission, the placebo effect, *vis medicatrix naturae*, careless reporting of the facts, and so on. But what has happened to the heart and mind and spirit of the individual healed, and what the practitioner on the case may have seen and understood and felt while praying—these are experiential data quite beyond the cynic's comprehension or calibration.

One pattern familiar to many Christian Science practitioners is that of "working" metaphysically on a difficult case for an extended period of time without results, until one day as they reach out to God with all their heart a sudden influx of light reveals the specific "truth" they need to know—and an immediate healing takes place. Many Christian Scientists who are not practitioners have had a similar experience in connection with their own working out of a problem—so much so that in later years they are likely to think not "That was the time I was healed of pneumonia," but "That was the time I learned what real humility is" or "That was the time I saw so clearly that all power belongs to God."[10] This effectively distinguishes the prayer of Christian healing from mental techniques of suggestion or psychological manipulation. Prayer reaches out for truth, not merely for well-being.

This is illustrated in the testimony of a woman who turned to Christian Science after the doctor told her he could do no more for her. Suffering from an internal growth, totally blind, almost completely paralyzed, and finally in a semicoma, she heard her husband say to the practitioner who had been called in, "If Christian Science heals my wife, I'll be the best Christian Scientist you have in your organization." The practitioner answered: "Don't say that. If Christian Science is not the truth, you do not want it, even if it heals her. If it is the truth, you want it, even if she is not healed." Suddenly, as the woman later explained, "the fear of dying left me in my realization that what I really wanted was to know God better—to know Him as He actually is—to know the truth." The same night she was instantaneously healed.[11] For the past thirty-seven years she has been carrying on the healing work as a full-time Christian Science practitioner.

The metaphysical basis on which the practitioner's prayer rests is the often quoted "scientific statement of being" in *Science and Health:*

> There is no life, truth, intelligence, nor substance in matter. All is infinite Mind and its infinite manifestation, for God is All-in-all. Spirit is immortal Truth; matter is mortal error. Spirit is the real and eternal; matter is the unreal and temporal. Spirit is God, and man is His image and likeness. Therefore man is not material; he is spiritual.[12]

This is, so to speak, the bare bones or ontological framework of Christian Science treatment, but vastly more than mere intellectual assertion or even fervent affirmation is required if the Word is to be made flesh in concrete healing. Christianity at its best has always known that the letter without the spirit kills rather than saves, and a Christianity that is merely a system of belief rather than a way of life is bound for extinction. At the same time a scientific theory that cannot be validated by experiment or experience may be interesting but hardly convincing. Combining those two necessities, Eddy wrote:

> St. Paul said to the Athenians, "For in Him we live, and move, and have our being." This statement is in substance identical with my own: "There is no life, truth, substance, nor intelligence in matter." It is quite clear that as yet this grandest verity has not been fully demonstrated, but it is nevertheless true. If Christian Science reiterates St. Paul's teaching, we, as Christian Scientists, should give to the world convincing proof of the validity of this scientific statement of being. Having perceived, in advance of others, this scientific fact, we owe to ourselves and to the world a struggle for its demonstration. [13]

This is why Christian Science is both a study and a practice. On many occasions Eddy used such terms as Divine Science, the Science of Being, and the Science of Mind to describe the divine Mind's own understanding of itself and its spiritual creation—language that reminds one of thirteenth-century scholasticism's bifurcated Divine Science and Science of God. The term Christian Science, Eddy explained, was synonymous with these other terms but related especially to "Science as applied to humanity."[14] And this is the point at which definition demands action, commitment, *results*. In the words of *Science and Health*, "Science will declare God aright, and Christianity will demonstrate this declaration and its divine Principle, making mankind better physically, morally, and spiritually."[15]

Here was an open invitation to the pragmatic test.

HEALTH

In general, Christian Scientists give considerably less attention to their physical health than most people—though the attention that the more earnest of them give to moral and spiritual health may sometimes rival the zeal of the Puritan ancestors of their founder. In line with this, the founder herself wrote:

Healing physical sickness is the smallest part of Christian Science. It is only the bugle-call to thought and action, in the higher range of infinite goodness. The emphatic purpose of Christian Science is the healing of sin; and this task, sometimes, may be harder than the cure of disease; because, while mortals love to sin, they do not love to be sick.[16]

The fact that Christian Scientists eschew alcohol, tobacco, and drugs— some of them extending this to rejection of tea and coffee—is therefore to be understood as a moral rather than a physical health measure. It is part of a desire to be as independent of matter as possible. Even excessive reliance on exercise, diet, or fresh air is regarded as making a little god of what should be regarded as merely a normal, balanced way of living. "Moderation in all things" would probably hold true for most Christian Scientists—a motto that brings to mind Emerson's indictment of the "pale negatives of Boston Unitarianism"—but for many Christian Scientists such moderation is counterbalanced by a spiritual commitment so radical that they are willing to stake their lives on the reality and power of Spirit.

Later chapters in this book examine more closely the caring and curing activities of Christian Science as an organized movement. But there is little likelihood of understanding these practical aspects of the subject unless one first grasps something of the basic spirit of the denomination's healing ministry.

In some degree every Christian Scientist is expected to be a practitioner. Not all of them as professionals, of course, with names listed in the directory of practitioners in the monthly *Christian Science Journal*—but at least as individuals striving to let more of the Christ-spirit shine with its healing power through their private lives and relations with others.

To enter into the full-time public practice of Christian Science is a step to be taken only as a result of profound commitment, study, discipline, prayer, and spiritual growth. For listing in the *Journal* directory one must give evidence of Christian character, a moral life, devotion to Christian Science, and freedom from other business or professional commitments, as well as furnishing detailed testimonies of healing from individuals outside one's own family who have turned to one for help in cases of severe illness or disability.

A practitioner is not per se an officer, spokesperson, or agent of the church, although he or she, like any other church member, may be elected to a temporary office. Some practitioners are appointed to serve on the church's board of lectureship for a period, a few become teachers of Christian Science as well as practitioners, but the great majority devote their full time to the healing work—and make their living by it.

Some people are shocked that these practitioners are "paid for their prayers"—an inexact statement, since what they are actually being paid for is the time, preparation, study, discipline, and spiritual preparedness they bring to their prayers. The remuneration is usually very modest in comparison with today's astronomical medical costs and charges. For many Christian Scientists who leave successful business or professional positions to enter the healing practice, the step involves a considerable financial sacrifice and demands a firm faith that they will be able (in Christian Science jargon) to "demonstrate supply." The contrasting experiences of two close friends of mine may throw more light on this subject than any mere exposition of theory could do.

One of these friends was an Englishman who became a Christian Science practitioner early in the Great Depression of the 1930s. Although he was strikingly successful in his healing work, the financial stringencies of that period were so acute that none of his patients seemed able to pay him. He prayed faithfully about the situation, but without apparent effect.

Then one day a very wealthy man asked him for Christian Science treatment for his chronically ill teenage daughter. Over several years the girl—steadily wasting away and by then wholly immobilized—had been taken to the best clinics in England and on the Continent in a vain search for healing. My friend gave one "treatment"—that is, he prayed until he could see clearly her spiritual perfection as the child of God—and the girl was healed. The next day the exuberant father offered him a check for a thousand pounds sterling in payment. Here, it seemed, was a clear demonstration of "supply." But a quiet inner voice said no, and the practitioner told the father he could not accept the check; his charge for a single treatment was ten shillings. The father protested that a thousand pounds meant nothing to him; he had paid vastly more than that for the years of unsuccessful medical treatment. But my friend remained firm.

When describing this incident to me later, he told me that as the check was offered to him he saw in a flash that the father was grateful for the healing but didn't have the slightest idea that what he had encountered was the very gift of God: a new kind of reality, a new scale of values. Up to now he had been used to buying whatever he wanted; the one thing he hadn't been able to buy was his daughter's health. He must be helped to see that there was no cash equivalent for the healing Christ.

As this dawned on my friend, he realized with sudden relief, "Why, a thousand pounds doesn't mean any more to God than ten shillings!"—and the whole sense of financial burden simply dropped away. From then on every one of his patients was able to pay him, and his needs and his family's were amply met.

My other friend's experience also occurred during the Great Depression. At that time he was a well-established and well-to-do practitioner. One day a shabby, emaciated man, barely able to walk, came to his office and asked for help. He was unemployed, the doctor had told him he had little time left to live, and his family was in a desperate situation. Hearing about Christian Science, he had decided to use one of his last two dimes to take a bus across the city to the building where he understood several Christian Science practitioners had offices. (That was the day of ten-cent bus fares!) My friend talked with him for about an hour. He told me later that he had never had anyone come to him for treatment who listened so wholeheartedly and drank in so thirstily all that he explained to him of God's boundless love for him, and what that meant. When the man left, full of gratitude, he offered his last dime to my friend, apologizing that he could give so little for what he had received. The practitioner's first impulse was to hand him a ten-dollar bill for his immediate need. But in this case too an inner voice said no, and he asked himself, "Can you possibly have less faith than this man?"

The next morning the man turned up again, eager to tell his story. After leaving the office the day before, he had started on the long walk home, his thoughts full of what he had been hearing about God and his own true being. Halfway there he suddenly realized that he was walking with perfect ease and normal strength. In short, he was healed. Then, as he hurried on to tell his family the good news, he ran into a friend he hadn't seen for several years. As soon as the friend learned of his unemployment, he offered him a position that had just become vacant in his own firm. In telling this the next day to my practitioner friend, the man looked almost literally transfigured, but his greatest joy (my friend reported) was obviously in the new sense of being he had discovered.

These two episodes—one involving the acceptance of a poor man's last dime, and one the rejection of a rich man's offer of a thousand pounds—are more than fancy anecdotes or pious parables. They are real events, unusual but not unrepresentative of what might be expected of a Christian Science practitioner in either situation. The practitioner's role is basically one of Christian ministry. There are degrees of selflessness and dedication to be found among those engaged in this spiritual healing work, as there are among physicians and pastors. Consecration demands constant spiritual growth, a willingness to learn from experience as well as from study, prayer, and inspiration. Probably most practitioners have had moments of stress and challenge when they have had to turn with simple trust to the words of Eddy's best-loved hymn "Feed my Sheep":

Shepherd, show me how to go
O'er the hillside steep,
How to gather, how to sow,—
How to feed Thy sheep;
I will listen for Thy voice,
Lest my footsteps stray;
I will follow and rejoice
All the rugged way. [17]

Rugged, yes. But from my own experience I can think of no greater joy than seeing lives transformed by the shepherding love and healing power of the ever-present Christ. People want healing, but even more they want truth. The two are not unrelated. Healing, for the Christian Scientist, is more than a rescue from pain or disability; it is a revelation, in some degree, of what Jesus meant when he said, "I am the way, the *truth*, and the life" (John 14:6). The practitioner is committed to helping each person who comes for healing to find his or her true selfhood as the child of God.

Karl Barth has written of the Christian ministry with typically fierce eloquence:

> Is it true, this talk of a loving and good God, who is more than one of the friendly idols whose rise is so easy to account for, and whose dominion is so brief? What the people want to find out and thoroughly understand is, *Is it true?* . . . Let us not be surprised that this want of theirs seldom or never meets us openly with such urgency as I have indicated. People naturally do not shout it out. . . . They expect us to understand them better than they understand themselves. . . . We are unfeeling, not when we probe deeply into the wound which they carry when they come to us for healing, but rather when we pass over it as if we did not know why they had come. We are misled not when we assume that they are brought to us by the last and profoundest questions, but rather when we think that when they come to us they may really be put off with next-to-the-last and less profound answers. [18]

The Christian Science practitioner is committed to answering calls for help at all hours of the day or night—not merely with comforting words but also with prayer that probes to the heart of the problem. The cry "Is it really true?" must be answered out of a life devoted to proving the truth of God's infinitely powerful love. And it demands, in addition to patience and courage, the humility that can say with Jesus, "I can of mine own self do *nothing*: . . . the Father that dwelleth in me, he doeth the works" (John 5:30; 14:10).

·6·

Mortality, Suffering, Madness, Malice

For we know that the whole creation groaneth and travaileth in pain together until now. And not only they, but ourselves also, which have the firstfruits of the Spirit, even we ourselves groan within ourselves, waiting for the adoption, to wit, the redemption of our body.

—*Romans 8:22–23*

MORTALITY

One way of looking at the account of the creation and fall of the human race in chapters two and three of Genesis is to see it as the mythic representation of a supposedly divine experiment that turned out to be an ungodly miscalculation. Unlike the first chapter's vision of a majestic, universal order in which everything made is "very good," the Eden allegory posits a fatally flawed world in which humankind is endowed from the beginning with a built-in capacity to err. This in turn suggests a creator with a little less wisdom and foresight than is found in Murphy's jokingly rueful but metaphysically challenging "law": If a thing *can* go wrong, it *will* go wrong.

Translated from biblical allegory to evolutionary theory, the problem remains. In the present rather absurd quarrel between "creationist science" and the scientific establishment, Christian Scientists find themselves unable to agree with either party. For both assume the ontological reality of the physical world as mortals perceive it. Christian Science, contrariwise, proceeds from the basic conviction that reality is wholly spiritual, tangible and present to spiritual sense, but clouded, distorted, even reversed by the false supposition that matter is the source of life and consciousness.

Only four years after the publication of Darwin's *Descent of Man*, Eddy wrote in the first edition of *Science and Health*, "Mr. Darwin is right with regard to mortal man or matter, but should have made a distinction between these and the immortal, whose basis is spirit."[1] Later she wrote:

> Mortals are the counterfeits of immortals. They are the children of the wicked one, or the one evil, which declares that man begins in dust or as a material embryo. . . . Mortals are not fallen children of God. They never had a perfect state of being, which may subsequently be regained. They were, from the beginning of mortal history, "conceived in sin and brought forth in iniquity." . . . Learn this, O mortal, and earnestly seek the spiritual status of man, which is outside of all material selfhood. . . . Jesus beheld in Science the perfect man, who appeared to him where sinning mortal man appears to mortals. In this perfect man the Saviour saw God's own likeness, and this correct view of man healed the sick. Thus Jesus taught that the kingdom of God is intact, universal, and that man is pure and holy. . . .
>
> Through discernment of the spiritual opposite of materiality, even the way through Christ, Truth, man will reopen with the key of divine Science the gates of Paradise which human beliefs have closed, and will find himself unfallen, upright, pure, and free. . . .[2]

In the vast evolutionary panorama of organic life as mortals perceive it, two facts stand out: the persistent innovative thrust of nature toward higher intelligence, and the stupendous cruelty, waste, and suffering involved in the process. Emerson celebrated the thrust toward intelligence in his striking pre-Darwinian lines: "And, striving to be man, the worm / Mounts through all the spires of form."[3] But Herman Melville, recoiling from the inhumanity and materialism of a Gilded Age that used (and largely misinterpreted) Darwinism's survival of the fittest to justify its ruthless capitalist struggles, commented ironically: "Found a family, build a state, / The pledged event is still the same: / Matter in end will never abate / His ancient brutal claim."[4]

Today matter and mind are widely regarded as a continuum rather than as two separate entities connected in some mysterious way that no one from Descartes to the modern neurologist has been able to explain satisfactorily. To the neurologist it remains an article of sheer faith that the electrochemistry of the brain actually translates itself into conceptual thinking. To the philosophical idealist the theory that matter is a construct of consciousness remains just that—a theory. But both can agree that matter "in the old sense" has "ceased to exist."[5]

I can remember how startled I was as a Harvard freshman in 1928 when one of my professors, Kirtley Mather, a respected geologist as well as a prominent evangelical layman and a bit of a wag to boot, described matter as "nothing, moving very quickly," a definition soon transformed by his students into "nothing going nowhere in a hurry."

Since that time there has been prolonged and brilliantly daring speculation among top-level physicists as to the reality, unreality, or semireality (that is, mere potentiality) of the quantum world underlying the "commonsense" world of appearances. But despite the growing corpus of professional and popularized literature on the subject, society as a whole has been slow to recognize the profound implications of the quantum revolution and the "reality crisis" it has led to in the physics community. This intellectual indifference has been especially notable in the fields of biology, neurology, and biomedicine. As the English physicist Paul Davies has said, "It is ironical that physics, which has led the way for all other sciences, is now moving towards a more accommodating view of mind, while the life sciences, following the path of last century's physics, are trying to abolish mind altogether." And he goes on to quote the explanation given by Harold Morowitz, a psychologist:

> What has happened is that biologists, who once postulated a privileged role for the human mind in nature's hierarchy, have been moving relentlessly toward the hard-core materialism that characterized nineteenth-century physics. At the same time physicists, faced with compelling experimental evidence, have been moving away from strictly mechanical models of the universe to a view that sees the mind as playing an integral role in all physical events.[6]

Theology also has been slow to recognize and explore the implications of this changing view of the mind-matter relationship. And here it must be noted that for Christian Scientists the basic distinction is not between mind and matter, which they see as merely opposite faces of the same counterfeit coin, but between mortal mind and the divine Mind, God. The important question for them is not so much epistemological as ontological and deeply religious, but also very practical. A paragraph in *Science and Health* relates this further to the problem of theodicy:

> When we endow matter with vague spiritual power,—that is, when we do so in our theories, for of course we cannot really endow matter with what it does not and cannot possess,—we disown the Almighty, for such theories lead to one of two things. They either presuppose the self-evolution and self-government of matter, or else they assume that matter is the product of Spirit. To seize the first horn of this dilemma and consider

matter as a power in and of itself, is to leave the creator out of His own universe; while to grasp the other horn of the dilemma and regard God as the creator of matter, is not only to make Him responsible for all disasters, physical and moral, but to announce Him as their source, thereby making Him guilty of maintaining perpetual misrule in the form and under the name of natural law.[7]

Even at best, as Christian Scientists see it, matter is limitation. Mortality is inherent in its very nature. Whatever is material must sometime perish from its own inadequacy. Waste and ultimate failure are written into the scenario of the whole evolutionary pageant of organic life on this brief planet. Alas, poor Adam!—to be saddled with the blame! If God created matter, must he not be held responsible for its "brutal claim" to set sharp limits on the spiritual possibilities of the human race?

Pointing out that in the Eden allegory Yahweh cast Adam into a deep, hypnotic sleep, *Science and Health* figuratively describes the whole of mortal existence as the "Adam-dream" induced by a false sense of God's nature and man's origin—a dream that can at any moment turn into nightmare. But what the book characterizes as the "ghastly farce of material existence"[8] is not to be tidied up by an act of will or legerdemain; the need is for an awakening to the actual facts of being as God perceives them. In less figurative language Eddy asks:

What is man? Brain, heart, blood, bones, etc., the material structure? If the real man is in the material body, you take away a portion of the man when you amputate a limb; the surgeon destroys manhood, and worms annihilate it. But the loss of a limb or injury to a tissue is sometimes the quickener of manliness; and the unfortunate cripple may present more nobility than the statuesque athlete,—teaching us by his very deprivations, that "a man's a man, for a' that."

When we admit that matter (heart, blood, brain, acting through the five physical senses) constitutes man, we fail to see how anatomy can distinguish between humanity and the brute, or determine when man is really *man* and has progressed farther than his animal progenitors. . . .

The name Adam represents the false supposition that Life is not eternal, but has beginning and end; that the infinite enters the finite, that intelligence passes into non-intelligence, and that Soul dwells in material sense; that immortal Mind results in matter, and matter in mortal mind; that the one God and creator entered what He created, and then disappeared in the atheism of matter.[9]

This is the background of thought against which Christian Science places the uniquely meaningful birth, life, healing ministry, crucifixion, and resurrection of Jesus, including also his final ascension beyond any possibility of perception by the material senses.

SUFFERING

Several years ago a teenage Christian Scientist was invited to give a talk on his religious beliefs to an evangelical youth group in his town. After presenting a highly idealized picture of the peace, well-being, and immunity from all unpleasantness that Christian Scientists supposedly enjoy, he was asked among other questions, "But don't you believe that Jesus *suffered* on the cross?" Clearly flummoxed, he mumbled after a painful pause, "Well, I think he was *uncomfortable*." That was as much weakness as he could admit in so godly a figure.

As the story got around among Christian Scientists, it caused a certain amount of mirth mixed with horror. One kindly person suggested that the young positive thinker study the chapter "Atonement and Eucharist" in *Science and Health* and ponder its deeply moving portrayal of the Saviour's supreme sacrifice. The chapter abounds in references to the "agony" and "suffering" of this "man of sorrows" who "bore our sins in his body," to the "earthly cup of bitterness" he "drained to the dregs," to his anguished struggle in Gethsemane, to the "pangs of neglect" and the "staves of bigoted ignorance" that smote him as he bent beneath the burden of an hour "terrible beyond human conception"—a burden which, at the last moment of "mockery, desertion, torture," wrung from his lips "the awful cry, 'My God, why hast Thou forsaken me?'"[10]

Yet none of this suffering is viewed in *Science and Health* as imposed by God on his beloved Son. On the contrary, it is seen as emanating from the "carnal" or mortal mind which is "enmity against God." The fundamental or original sin of this mortal mentality is understood to be its spurious claim to an existence separate from the infinite Life that is God, Spirit. In Augustinian terms, the devil is the ape of God. Jesus, also personalizing the source of all evil in a vivid metaphor, reduced it to mere imposture and sham when he said of the mythical prince of darkness: "He was a murderer from the beginning, and abode not in the truth, because there is no truth in him. When he speaketh a lie, he speaketh of his own: for he is a liar, and the father of it" (John 8:44).

To a Christian Scientist, disease, poverty, accident, suffering, madness, injustice, death—evil of every sort—proceed from a false sense of the origin of life. Physical humanity is to be seen as a misconception of true (spiritual) being. All suffering arises from this "original" sin. God does not send disease and disaster as a punishment for particular sins, but erroneous belief or wrong action of any sort—conscious or unconscious, willful or induced— brings its own penalty upon itself until recognized and relinquished.

"The procuring cause and foundation of all sickness," Eddy wrote, "is fear, ignorance, or sin." Psychologically the three are closely related, and the word *sin* in its metaphysical rather than its moral sense covers all three. At this deeper level Eddy could write that "suffering is an error of sinful sense which Truth destroys, and . . . eventually both sin and suffering will fall at the feet of everlasting Love."[11]

This is the part of Christian Science least understood by its critics, for it hinges on the basic distinction between the "real man" (generic) and imperfect mortals. Take, for instance, the sentence in *Science and Health:* "Man is incapable of sin, sickness, and death."[12] If taken out of context, this is easy to dismiss as both shocking and nonsensical. But the next sentence continues, "The real man cannot depart from holiness, nor can God, by whom man is evolved, engender the capacity or freedom to sin," and this is followed by "A mortal sinner is not God's man."

Then what *is* this man, using the term to include both the male and female of God's creating?

Christian Science answers that it was the mission of Jesus of Nazareth to show the world once and for all what each of us as a child of God really is, and to do this by exemplification. Through him we glimpse the eternal Christman or Christ-idea constituted and governed by Spirit and wholly free from the bonds of the flesh. This was the intolerable blessing he brought to a world afraid to let go of its mortal limitations, and for this he was crucified.

Here we reach another aspect of the problem of suffering—the suffering for *others'* sins. Jesus "bore our sins in his body." Every true Christian who cares deeply about the sins and woes of the world must learn through experience something of what that means. As Eddy put it,

> Remembering the sweat of agony which fell in holy benediction on the grass of Gethsemane, shall the humblest or mightiest disciple murmur when he drinks from the same cup, and think, or even wish, to escape the exalting ordeal of sin's revenge on its destroyer? . . .

> Forsaken by all whom he [Jesus] had blessed, this faithful sentinel of God at the highest post of power, charged with the grandest trust of heaven, was ready to be transformed by the renewing of the infinite Spirit. He was to prove that the Christ is not subject to material conditions, but is above the reach of human wrath, and is able, through Truth, Life, and Love, to triumph over sin, sickness, death, and the grave.[13]

At this point Christian Science parts company decisively with today's theological trend toward interpreting the crucifixion in terms of God's sharing through his son in the unspeakable sufferings he is presumed to have permitted in his creation through eons of evolution. As a writer in the *Christian Century* in 1986 summed it up coolly, "The ancient theopaschite heresy that God suffers has, in fact, become the new orthodoxy."[14] Behind it is a growing assumption that the creator is limited in power but strong in sympathy, a view well represented by Whitehead's statement that God is "the fellow-sufferer who understands."[15] And perhaps the classic expression of the new orthodoxy is Bonhoeffer's bald statement: "Our God is a suffering God. Suffering forms man into the image of God. The suffering man is in the likeness of God."[16]

There is undoubtedly a desperate comfort to be drawn from this focus on what is increasingly called "the suffering God on the cross." But to some it seems a far cry from the ringing joy of primitive Christianity, with its confident greeting, "The Lord is risen." In dropping the omnipotence of a God who is infinite Love, it surrenders also the possibility of the resurrection of Jesus Christ as literal fact. Embarrassed by the "naive" apostolic faith that the Christ has indeed "abolished death, and . . . brought life and immortality to light through the gospel," a deeply troubled theology in a world of holocaust and scientific savagery finds what comfort it can from deifying suffering. That, at least, is the way a Christian Scientist might see what to many others seems a nobly tragic realism.

Meanwhile medical research and social reform seek to eliminate or alleviate human suffering as much as possible, by means unknown to Jesus but, some might say, unnecessary to him in his supreme victory over the mortality that includes all suffering, all materiality. Christian Science sees in that central event of human history the promise of ultimate victory over every last claim of evil to presence and power.

In one of the ecumenical discussions mentioned at the beginning of Chapter 2, the subject centered on the various participants' views of the resurrection. The Christian Science representatives found that on this topic they were considerably more orthodox than any of the mainline representatives present. On the basis of their experience of healing, they had no difficulty in accepting the resurrection as a historic event, concrete in time and place. Although the various Gospel accounts differ considerably in detail, the general tenor is perfectly clear, they felt. As their position paper put it:

> The risen Jesus walked and talked and ate, using mouth, hands, feet. He
> provided the physical evidence of identity asked by Thomas. Between
> resurrection and ascension he had unique control over this physique, but it
> was no apparition; it was human flesh and bone. Resurrection may prop-
> erly be used as a metaphor to designate individual awakening from an
> earthly material sense of existence to a higher spiritual sense of living. But
> the resurrection of Jesus was not a metaphor or a myth or a mere psychic
> experience of his disciples. . . . Step by step he had demonstrated the
> spiritual authority of the Christ over a physical sense of life. His own
> resurrection was the logical crown to this progressive demonstration.[17]

This rather dry statement rests on something more than blind faith or
fundamentalist literalism. As the position paper goes on to point out, the
resurrection did not occur as an isolated fact; it needs to be seen in the full
context of Jesus' healing and saving mission. This is where Christian healers
and those who have experienced this kind of healing in what many people
might consider a miraculous way bring to the Gospel record an added
element of understanding and conviction. The position paper relates this fact
to the whole question of New Testament healing:

> Christian Scientists are satisfied that they have good grounds for accept-
> ing in full the healing record of Jesus. For us it is an integral part of the
> founding of basic Christianity. Furthermore, in our own experience we
> have seen the Christ exercising its authority over physical conditions. We
> have seen mental and emotional disorders cured; many of us have seen
> serious organic diseases healed. Some have seen beloved relatives and
> friends restored to health and vigor after medical opinion has judged death
> to be imminent or even already present. We are not acquainted with this
> healing work just by hearsay. We bear witness to that "which we have seen
> with our eyes, which we have looked upon, and our hands have handled, of
> the Word of life."[18]

This says nothing of the yearning compassion that is vital to all genuine
Christian healing. However, while *Science and Health* makes plain that the
suffering induced by mortal sense may often serve to turn thought toward
Spirit, it also makes clear the need for the utmost Christian concern for the
sufferer. This is summed up in a crucial passage in the chapter "Christian
Science Practice":

> If we would open their prison doors for the sick, we must first learn to
> bind up the broken-hearted. If we would heal by the Spirit, we must not
> hide the talent of spiritual healing under the napkin of its form, nor bury
> the *morale* of Christian Science in the grave-clothes of its letter. The
> tender word and Christian encouragement of an invalid, pitiful patience

with his fears and the removal of them, are better than hecatombs of gushing theories, stereotyped borrowed speeches, and the doling of arguments, which are but so many parodies on legitimate Christian Science, aflame with divine Love.[19]

This states the ideal. It is one more reminder that the letter killeth, but the spirit giveth life.

MADNESS

According to the Gospel narratives, a good part of Jesus' healing ministry consisted of casting out demons, among them the unclean spirit who announced, "My name is Legion; for we are many." Today the names have changed, but they are still many. They range from common stress to anxiety neurosis to manic-depressive psychosis, with a vast variety of mental ills between and beyond. We no longer believe in demons, but our deeply disturbed century has seen the word *demonic* once more come into favor.

At the same time we worship at the twin shrines of physical fitness and mental health, with millions of worshippers unaware of the vital connection between the two. Oddly enough, Christian Scientists and psychoanalysts are among those who are most acutely aware of the link, although they differ radically in both theory and therapy. With the spectacular development of biomedicine and now of cellular pathology, psychoanalysis has been losing ground and psychiatry has been turning back increasingly to the physiological and neuropathic aspects of mental illness, with a resultant emphasis on drugs and surgery.

In the light of this development, there is a new timeliness in several statements in *Science and Health* which seem to imply that the root "belief" to be handled in a case of insanity is a physiological rather than a psychological one. While all diseases and suffering are held to be mental and to arise from false belief, the difference is that "insanity implies belief in a diseased brain, while physical ailments (so-called) arise from the belief that other portions of the body are deranged." Derangement, or *disarrangement*, the statement continues, "is a word which conveys the true definition of all human belief in ill-health, or disturbed harmony."[20]

This discussion occurs in a part of *Science and Health* dealing with the mental "arguments" a practitioner may find helpful in treating a patient. The argument is not with the patient but with the erroneous patterns of human belief and the false evidence of material sense that would try to define the situation to be healed. If used at all, it is usually a silent process within the practitioner's thought. Like the lawyer defending a client from false charges based on spurious evidence, the practitioner will reach out for the true (spiritual) facts that bear irrefutable witness to the patient's innocence as the child of God. On that basis the case may be appealed to what *Science and Health* describes as the Supreme Court of Spirit, where no further argument is necessary, for, in the words of Revelation 12, "Now is come salvation, and strength, and the kingdom of our God, and the power of his Christ: for the accuser of our brethren is cast down, which accused them before our God day and night."

The reasoning processes described as argument, *Science and Health* makes clear, are to be regarded only as "human auxiliaries to aid in bringing thought into accord with the spirit of Truth and Love, which heals the sick and the sinner." This casts light on another key passage in the same book:

> The treatment of insanity is especially interesting. However obstinate the case, it yields more readily than do most diseases to the salutary action of truth, which counteracts error. The arguments to be used in curing insanity are the same as in other diseases: namely, the impossibility that matter, brain, can control or derange mind, can suffer or cause suffering; also the fact that truth and love will establish a healthy state, guide and govern mortal mind or the thought of the patient, and destroy all error, whether it is called dementia, hatred, or any other discord.[21]

Christian Science history includes healings of a variety of psychological ills, extending from violent insanity to suicidal depression, alcoholism, drug addiction, sexual aberration, kleptomania, and xenophobia (I list only ones I have known about personally). But some practitioners have been puzzled when they have found in their experience that insanity has not "yielded more readily" than most diseases. Perhaps because of the emphasis on psychology in this century they have been unconsciously influenced to think of mental illness as supposedly caused by nurture (external circumstance and experience) more than by genetic factors or brain damage. In that case, according to Eddy's statement, their denials and affirmations might not be getting at the root of the error, namely, the belief in life, consciousness, and causation in matter.

A passage in *A Century of Christian Science Healing* makes this point:

> When the skeptics of Jesus' day insisted that he healed—"cast out devils"—by Beelzebub, the prince of the devils, his reply indicated that this might indeed be the method used by some of his critics. "But," he added, "if I cast out devils by the Spirit of God, then the kingdom of God is come unto you" (Matthew 12:28).

Instead of rejecting this as a reference to an obsolete demonology, the Christian Scientist sees in it a figurative description of two ways of handling the evils that bedevil human existence. One way would use the powers of the human mind to control the evils arising from the human mind's own shortcomings. The other way endeavors simply to "let this mind be in you, which was also in Christ Jesus" (Phil. 2:5)—and understands this to be the eternal Mind or Spirit called God. [22]

Since Christian Science sees all disease as mental, it is not surprising that it does not draw a sharp line of distinction between mental and physical illness. In the same way its perception of both sickness and sin as a delusive sense of being means that its basic approach to the healing of insanity is not radically different from its spiritual therapy in a case, say, of measles or marital infidelity. A few sentences from *Science and Health* indicate the broad implications of this position:

> There are many species of insanity. All sin is insanity in different degrees. Sin is spared from this classification, only because its method of madness is in consonance with common mortal belief. . . . Those unfortunate people who are committed to insane asylums are only so many distinctly defined instances of the baneful effects of illusion on mortal minds and bodies. [23]

There may be a sense in which all of us, to the extent that we are deluded by material appearances and assumptions, are a little less than sane, as we intermittently recognize. This recognition shows up casually in our use of the word *mad* to describe everything from the picturesque eccentricities of a retired Oxford professor ("A delightful chap—but quite mad, you know!") to the unspeakable recklessness of a nuclear arms race barely if at all held in check by the threat of cataclysmic mutual assured destruction, with its apt acronym MAD. Eddy was well aware that her own teachings would be considered mad if they were divorced from their practical results in living. In an 1886 message to her church she wrote:

> Metaphysics, not physics, enables us to stand erect on sublime heights, surveying the immeasurable universe of Mind, peering into the cause which governs all effects, while we are strong in the unity of God and man. There is "method" in the "madness" of this system,—since madness it seems to many onlookers. This method sits serene at the portals of the temple of thought, while the leaders of materialistic schools indulge in mad antics. [24]

Interestingly enough, physics itself was on the brink of a revolution that would seem like "mad antics" to the mechanistic world of Newtonian logic but actually was moving away from the materialism of the past and opening up toward the "immeasurable universe" of mind. In 1896 the French physicist Antoine-Henri Becquerel discovered radioactivity; the next year J. J. Thomson discovered the electron; the following year the Curies discovered radium. The new era in physics had begun, although quantum theory and the complementarity and uncertainty principles lay some years ahead.

For the time being, science as a whole and society at large still remained snugly anchored in the materialistic determinism of the past three centuries, with its inherent challenge to the spiritual premise of Christianity. But the challenge was reciprocal. As early as 1898 Eddy had chosen the topic "Is the universe, including man, evolved by atomic force?" for systematic study by Christian Scientists for two weeks every year. There was, it appeared, definite method in her "madness."

Ironically, the charge of madness was actually brought against her in 1907 in the notorious "Next Friends suit," initiated by the *New York World* and given sensational prominence in the national press. Ostensibly the case hinged on Eddy's alleged mental incompetence to manage her own affairs or protect her financial interests and property rights from misappropriation by those around her. But the opening argument before the court by ex-Senator William E. Chandler of Concord, chief attorney for the plaintiffs, disclosed a very different purpose. *Science and Health* alone, Chandler announced, was proof that Eddy suffered from various "systematized delusions and dementia."[25]

The suit itself collapsed ignominiously after the three masters appointed by the court to try the case examined Eddy in the library of her modest home and found, instead of the doddering, palsied "lunatic" they had been led to expect, a composed old lady with an alert mind who was clearly able to look after herself.[26] A day or two later Chandler, who had spent months preparing his case, with a retinue of lawyers, reporters, and psychologists, moved for dismissal of the suit without judgment, and the whole farce came to an end.

Although Eddy's intelligence had been vindicated, a question still remained regarding the rationality of her warnings against the malicious use of willpower and "aggressive mental suggestion"—which is what she meant by malicious animal magnetism. As Christian Scientists see it, this kind of subtle psychological manipulation of others' thinking is the antithesis of yielding to the divine Mind and letting God's will be done. It is a form of mental malpractice, hypnotic in action and rooted in self-will. Where used as a conscious, calculated technique it may lead finally to what Eddy called moral idiocy. But she drew a clear distinction between its malicious form and what she described as merely ignorant animal magnetism.[27]

The remedy for all such attacks, she taught, was to let the pure sunlight of Truth and Love shine down on the situation and disclose the dark corners of thought to be swept clean. But the malice of the carnal mind that Paul defined as enmity against God was not to be destroyed by shutting one's eyes to its "mad antics."

MALICE

In the quiet gentility of his Concord home, Emerson had written in the nineteenth century: "There is no pure lie, no pure malignity in nature. The entertainment of the proposition of depravity is the last profligacy and profanation. There is no scepticism, no atheism but that. Could it be received into common belief, suicide would unpeople the planet."[28]

A Christian Scientist might agree with this if the word *nature* in the first sentence were changed or interpreted to mean *reality* or the spiritual universe of God's creating. But as an interpretation of unredeemed human nature or mortal history it would have to be rejected as, frankly, eyewash. By contrast there is an almost shocking realism in the following passage from *Science and Health:*

> What a pitiful sight is malice, finding pleasure in revenge! Evil is sometimes a man's highest conception of right, until his grasp on good grows stronger. Then he loses pleasure in wickedness, and it becomes his torment. The way to escape the misery of sin is to cease sinning. There is no other way. Sin is the image of the beast to be effaced by the sweat of agony. It is a moral madness which rushes forth to clamor with midnight and tempest.[29]

Eddy's statement may be quite as unpalatable as Emerson's to a secularized society that has largely substituted psychopathology and psychiatry for Christian theology and ethics. But for Christians, at least, words like *malice, wickedness, sin,* and *moral madness* can still have meaning in relation to the starker horrors of this century. Whether psychopath or sinner, an Adolf Hitler (as we learned in the 1930s with a shock) could hypnotize a great nation and thereby terrorize a whole world.

When the demonic element in human life operates on the grand scale, it is easy to recognize the crucial role of aggressive mental suggestion and mass mesmerism—or animal magnetism, as Mesmer called the startling power of suggestion, later domesticated and renamed hypnosis. In his 1929 tale *Mario the Magician*, Thomas Mann produced a masterly indirect analysis of the psychological power of Mussolini in Fascist Italy by presenting a vivid picture of the mental domination of a summer resort audience by a sleazy stage hypnotist. But the real trick is to recognize the early symptoms of such mental domination, whether on a global stage or in a one-to-one encounter.

A handy example of the latter occurs in a little book entitled *Understanding Our Century* published in 1984 to commemorate the seventy-fifth anniversary of the *Christian Science Monitor*. The quotation that follows is drawn from the last section, "Religion's Emerging Role":

> Where religion weakens, it may not mean that religion disappears. It may only mean that false gods step in. Carl Jung, no enemy to religion, early in this period warned against the return of the more "horrible" ancient religions:
> "At any time," he wrote, "they may break in upon us with destructive force, in the form of mass-suggestion, for example."
> As early as 1923, one month before the famous beer hall *Putsch* in Munich, the *Monitor* ran a front-page interview with Adolf Hitler, the "Bavarian Mussolini." There he was—unknown to the world at large but "not to be regarded lightly," staring "hard" into the interviewer's face, making "excited gestures" with his hands, raising his voice until "he almost shouted," then giving himself away in a statement that he emphasized with careful deliberation:
> "What has been possible in Italy also is possible in Germany, where the German people, given a Mussolini, would fall down on their knees before him and worship him more than Mussolini ever has been worshipped in Italy."
> When Hitler finally came to power, the *Monitor* correspondent would be one of the first American journalists to be expelled from Germany. Later, in 1941, Christian Science itself would be banned from the Third Reich and many of its religious practitioners imprisoned.[30]

When malice or moral idiocy comes in the form of a Holocaust or a Gulag Archipelago, the world is forced to take notice of it, though many warning signs along the way may have been ignored. For Christians the greatest example of all occurred two thousand years ago when the concentrated malice of the carnal mind attempted to bury the light of the world once and for all in the emptiness, the dark nothingness, of an earthly tomb. But in varying ways Christians have found in that greatest of tragedies the greatest of promises. Something of what it means to Christian Scientists is suggested in a single packed paragraph by the founder of their church:

The last act of the tragedy on Calvary rent the veil of matter, and unveiled Love's great legacy to mortals: *Love forgiving its enemies.* This grand act crowned and still crowns Christianity: it manumits mortals; it translates love; it gives to suffering, inspiration; to patience, experience; to experience, hope; to hope, faith; to faith, understanding; and to understanding, Love triumphant![31]

·7·

Passage to the Light

For my thoughts are not your thoughts, neither are your ways my ways, saith the Lord. For as the heavens are higher than the earth, so are my ways higher than your ways, and my thoughts than your thoughts.

—Isaiah 55:8, 9

The passages of life are in these days explored by anthropology, sociology, psychology—and religion. Each has its own emphases, complexities, insights, vocabulary. Here as elsewhere the radical spirituality of Christian Science leads to a rather surprising approach.

"The measurement of life by solar years robs youth and gives ugliness to age," *Science and Health* announces briskly. "Time-tables of birth and death are so many conspiracies against manhood and womanhood." The one passage the book names specifically is "the passage from sense to Soul, from a material sense of existence to the spiritual"[1]—an adventurous process that can be undertaken at any stage of human development.

In general we think of mortal existence in linear terms, beginning with birth and ending with death. But the Christian concept of a new birth cuts clean across this horizontal movement, lifting thought vertically to a new plane of perception—to a new reality, even a new selfhood. Such a glimpse may bring a measure of transformation to whatever passage of human life or situational crisis one may be facing.

This has been a recognizable phenomenon through the centuries. Many Christians would be able to agree with this statement by Eddy: "The new birth is not the work of a moment. It begins with moments, and goes on with years; moments of surrender to God, of childlike trust and joyful adoption of good; moments of self-abnegation, self-consecration, heaven-born hope, and spiritual love."[2]

71

There might be less agreement—and some puzzlement—over her next statement:

> Time may commence, but it cannot complete, the new birth: eternity does this, for progress is the law of infinity. Only through the sore travail of mortal mind shall soul as sense be satisfied, and man awake in His likeness. What a faith-lighted thought is this! that mortals can lay off the "old man," until man is found to be the image of the infinite good that we name God, and the fulness of the stature of man in Christ appears.[3]

What this means to Christian Scientists may be shown best through examples that will also illustrate the importance Christian Science gives to experiential "testimony." For this purpose I have chosen a scattering of diverse examples from the familiar arc of birth, childhood, youth, mid-life, old age, and death.

Since a baby can hardly be expected to describe its own experience in being born, I have chosen for this initial (and literal) passage the comments of an obstetrician who has attended approximately two hundred Christian Science births over the years. The following excerpts are from a lengthy letter[4] he wrote to a Christian Science practitioner whom he came to know during that period:

> In the beginning I must admit there was apprehension by me as well as the hospital staff in regard to our Christian Science patients. This fear centered on imagined interference with our duties, a denial of our problems and possible legal entanglement. Our experience has been entirely contrary to these fears. Our Christian Science patients have at all times given careful consideration to our problems. In certain instances they have courteously declined, or legally waived, many examinations considered routine; thus they have taken upon themselves the responsibilities for these omissions. Their expression of gratitude toward the staff has gained the staff's understanding and devotion.

A word of explanation is needed at this point. Many Christian Scientists prefer to have a home delivery, when they can find a doctor or licensed midwife willing to come at the needed time. In such cases a Christian Science nurse is usually present also. For the sake of convenience some prefer a hospital delivery. A large number of deliveries are reported to have occurred without any special problems and sometimes to have been quite painless.

The obstetrician's letter goes on to say that when a problem did occur, an interval of time was usually requested in order to work out the problem through Christian Science, and most frequently "the situation then became resolved." So much was this the case, he added, that "the delivery room staff regarded these patients as behaving in quite a special way." Often an arrested labor, not expected to terminate for hours, "would advance to delivery in a few minutes after phone consultation between patient and practitioner." The letter continues with a description of a "memorable occasion" which the writer considered to be an "irrefutable" instance of the healing power of Christian Science:

> A student of Christian Science had been in active labor for several hours with adequate progress. On examination a shoulder was found to be presenting, making normal delivery impossible. This finding was confirmed by X-ray examination and a further admonition by the consulting radiologist that a vaginal delivery was clearly impossible. This situation was discussed with the patient, her husband and over the phone with the practitioner. A recommendation for immediate delivery by Caesarean section was made. The family requested a few moments alone together for silent prayer, after which I was requested to do whatever I felt was necessary. As it would require a short time to prepare surgery for the operation, the patient and her family used the time in prayerful application of the principles of Christian Science. Fifteen minutes later on the way to surgery the patient turned quickly to me and asked if I would please examine her again. Without question and with absolute certainty I knew that I would find the impossible: delivery had now become possible, and so it was. We barely had time to return the patient for a normal delivery. The radiologist reviewed his films when told of the outcome and presented textbook evidence to prove it was impossible.

The writer adds that he has seen many other healings of difficult obstetric situations in his working relations with Christian Scientists. There has been "perfect harmony" and "mutual respect" between him and these patients. One interesting point is that freedom of choice "has always been allowed by the practitioner to the patients and a full realization that in Christian Science a demonstration was a very individual thing and subject to the limits of one's understanding." It is revealing to see that the good doctor has unconsciously picked up the word *demonstration* from his Christian Science clients.

The two accounts that follow, dealing with children, are typical of hundreds of others in the Christian Science periodicals which show children actually and actively participating in the healing and rescuing process. The first appeared in the *Christian Science Sentinel* of September 22, 1986; the second in the *Sentinel* of October 7, 1985.

The writer of the first—James Llewellyn Heiland of Monterey, California—tells how, when he was a small boy, his parents enrolled him in a Christian Science Sunday school even though they themselves were not members of the church. His attendance was at first irregular, but he always felt a great sense of kindness and love from his teacher there and from the other pupils.

When he was only eight years old he woke up one morning and found it impossible to move. Terrified, he cried out; when his father saw the situation, he drove him at once to the local hospital. After a thorough examination and X rays, pneumonia and a collapsed lung were diagnosed, and surgery for the latter was scheduled for two days later. His account continues:

> I cannot tell you how afraid I was. I had to stay in the hospital, and after my parents went home I felt completely alone. The next day my parents visited me and explained to me why I would have to have an operation. Before long all three of us were crying.
>
> As I sat alone in my bed that night, I remembered this sentence written on the wall of the Christian Science Sunday School . . . "God is Love." I quietly prayed. I remembered my teacher telling us that God loves His children very much. So I asked God for help. I knew a loving God would never forget even one of His children. I felt very calm. Suddenly I sat up. I realized that the pain was completely gone. I was absolutely thrilled!
>
> The next morning members of the hospital staff came in to prepare me for surgery. I told them that I felt fine. They smiled and told me everything would be OK. . . . When [my dad] arrived some staff members told him that I was not cooperating.
>
> My dad came over to me, and I quietly told him that I felt fine. I will always be grateful that he listened to me. He asked to speak to the physician. The physician didn't believe my report and asked my dad if he could take another set of X-rays, which my dad agreed to. To the physician's amazement, the X-rays showed nothing wrong with the lung at all. I was soon released from the hospital and on my way home!

Following this healing there was no doubt in the boy's mind that Christian Science was the way for him. Through the years of adolescence he continued to attend the Sunday school and later had Christian Science class instruction. Also he joined The Mother Church and a branch church where, over the years, he served in a variety of positions. His concluding words wrap up this simple story with an equally simple comment:

> My favorite work is what I'm doing now—serving as Sunday School superintendent, and in the Sunday School I attended as a child. My own four

children enjoy regular attendance in this Sunday School. . . . The same sentence from the Bible is still on our wall: "God is Love."5

The writer of the next account—Jane W. Lacey of Fairhope, Alabama— expresses "boundless thanks" for the privilege of raising her six children in Christian Science. "God," she writes, "has been my source of strength, and theirs, all through their formative years, and we have experienced years of freedom and joy in learning about God through the study of this Science." The particular experience she recounts occurred a number of years ago when she had only four children, the oldest a daughter of ten.

Their house was built on a piece of property that had a deep drainage ditch at the back of the lot. The city had recently paved the ditch in a U shape of concrete, making it one of the area's main drainage avenues. The children enjoyed playing and wading there during and after light rains. On one occasion, during a somewhat heavier rainstorm, the children begged to be allowed to run down and see "how their ditch was doing." Unaware that the rain had caused a flash flood in the vicinity, their mother gave them permission but told them not to put even a toe into the water until she joined them in a few minutes.

As she started down, she was met by the ten-year-old daughter running toward the house and crying, "Mamma, where are my books?" (that is, the Bible and *Science and Health*). The girl then frantically explained that her little sister and one of her younger brothers had each put a foot in the water and been swept away. What followed is better told in the testifier's own words:

I ran toward the ditch, and the closer I got the louder the roar of the water became. I cannot describe the dread that I felt. When I reached the edge of the rushing, angry water, our other son was standing there in great fear. . . .

My next thought was to feel deeply grateful that our children had been taught both at home and in the Christian Science Sunday School that God was always with them, guiding and guarding them. I simply knew that they were aware of this right at that moment. I raced back to the house. There I told our daughter to call a Christian Science practitioner, tell him what had happened, and ask him to pray for us right away.

Through the study of Christian Science I had come to a firm realization that the human measurement of time is certainly not God's measurement. As the Apostle Paul wrote . . . "Now is the accepted time; behold, now is the day of salvation." So I clung to the realization that no matter what seemed to have happened, right now the children were in the loving care of their Father-Mother God.

Later she learned that all along the ditch, men were rapidly putting up sandbags to try to stop the violent flow of water. As her two children were swept wildly along, the men stopped their work to race to their aid but couldn't catch up. At that point large slabs of concrete were being forced to the surface by the pressure of the water. At the end of a city block the ditch took an extreme left turn, and the water was crashing into a retaining wall. Along this route the children were traveling.

Meanwhile the mother had got out the family car and driven to the end of the block. By the time she arrived she was feeling "a calmer certainty of God's presence with our children." When she reached the turning point in the ditch, several men there were exclaiming at what they repeatedly called "a miracle." To her it was simply confirmation of what she had been claiming in her prayer.

> When I looked across the roaring water, I saw our two children on the opposite bank. They had made the sharp turn, passed the retaining wall, and were clinging to two little vines hardly the size of pencils. . . . To me the children's rescue . . . was not a miracle; it was evidence of God's omnipresence. I will never forget my sense of awe and deep gratitude for this wonderful proof of God's love and power to care for His children under any human condition.
>
> Later, when I had the children at home . . . I asked both of these little ones separately about what they had done during their ordeal, and each responded with the same statements. Each told of coming to the top of the water and crying, "God is Love," before being pulled back under. When they had passed the sharp turn in the ditch, each had reached out and caught a little branch and then come to rest on the sandy bank. Until that time, neither had been aware that the other was in the water. Once again, enormous gratitude to God was uppermost in my thoughts.[6]

The next two accounts tell the experiences that brought two very different people into Christian Science as they passed from their late teens into their early twenties. Both of these I have known well in their later years.

Friedrich Preller of Berlin, Germany, was a Christian Science practitioner, teacher, and public lecturer when I first knew him in the 1950s. His wife Käthe had been a practitioner listed in the *Christian Science Journal* since the early 1920s and is still carrying on that healing work today. Both had been courageous anti-Nazis during World War II, Friedrich being imprisoned for a time until his wife almost miraculously secured his release. A little later their son Arno was assigned to a labor camp after refusing to participate in certain Hitler youth activities in his school. Arno emigrated afterward to the United States where he became a professor of German literature and linguistics at Colorado State University, until he resigned to give all his time to the healing work, later becoming like his father a Christian Science teacher and lecturer as well. Today Arno's son Scott, who is a devoted Christian Scientist, is serving as a Protestant chaplain in the U.S. Air Force.

The following account is from one of Friedrich Preller's lectures.[7] Although he told it in the third person, the experience he related was his own. When delivering the lecture, he customarily explained to his audience at the conclusion of his account that "the boy who was healed is the man who is speaking to you today."

The unnamed "boy" had learned of Christian Science when he was nineteen. Up to that time he (Preller) had prayed a great deal in the way he had been taught as a child. Within a few years he had lost his mother, his father, and his brother. He himself suffered a serious hip disease resulting from an accident, and doctors had declared his case incurable. Since his mother's death he had leaned more than ever on God for loving care, and in so doing his prayers underwent a change. He now prayed as his heart dictated, and he felt happier. His prayers, "evidencing a firm faith," made it easier for him to bear his loss and his physical suffering. He was confined to a hospital for fifteen months.

Preller bore all his sorrow with a certain dignity, believing that God had ordained this experience of suffering for him. The last time he was in the hospital the New Testament was his only literature. Not only did he read a chapter from the Gospels each day, he studied it. He was disconcerted as he discovered what he felt to be a difference between the biblical record and the sermons preached from the pulpit.

One day he was discharged as incurable and, in order to walk at all, was obliged to wear an orthopedic brace. His right leg was two inches shorter than his left leg. He continued to attend church, but the conflict regarding his faith increased, and very soon he was led to withdraw entirely from the church. But his communion with God increased, and his prayers were now a sincere desire for right guidance as expressed in the words of the Psalmist: "Search me, O God, and know my heart: try me, and know my thoughts: and see if there be any wicked way in me, and lead me in the way everlasting."

When, two weeks after the young man's withdrawal from the church, he learned of Christian Science, he felt without question that his prayer had been heard. He became acquainted with a Christian Scientist who, at his request, explained a few fundamental truths regarding this, to him, new religion. She told him in particular what Christian Science teaches about God and one's true spiritual unity with God. When he was alone again, he let these "few but mighty thoughts" do their work in his consciousness. Suddenly it was as though scales fell from the young man's eyes, Preller told his lecture audiences. What he had sought in prayer, sensed and felt through an earnest study of the Bible, but had expected only beyond the grave, became a present experience through that first contact with Christian Science.

Complete newness of life with "undreamed-of possibilities" unfolded for him. With a quickening of thought that made the physical become "of no significance" to him, he grasped for the first time what it means to be the child of God and thus be able to enjoy God's love, goodness, and presence. He was so preoccupied with cherishing his newly acquired understanding that when he went to bed and removed the brace from his body, he didn't even think of a physical healing. When he woke the next morning, he discovered that for the first time in five and a half years he could stand and walk without pain. About two weeks later his right leg had regained its normal length and strength.

Why was it, Preller asked his audiences, that this healing did not come to the young man until Christian Science had touched his consciousness, although there had previously been such strong faith and fervent prayer? Undoubtedly, he answered, it was because his belief that illness was in accordance with God's will had prevented such a demonstration. But now, he explained, the seed of Christian Science had fallen on prepared soil. A suddenly illuminated understanding of God, accompanied by deep joy, had made prayer capable of bringing results. This experience, he summed up, comprised three essential points of the Christian Scientist's faith: the influx of the Holy Spirit, the birth of the Christ in human consciousness, and the resurrection to a new life.

In sharp contrast with this experience is an autobiographical sketch written by Deborah Appleton Huebsch for a book in which fourteen Christian Scientists of widely differing backgrounds conveyed something of what their religion had meant to each of them in their respective life patterns.[8] I first knew Deborah Heubsch when she was still fairly new in Christian Science, and have since seen her become a full-time Christian Science practitioner, later taking on the added responsibilities of a Christian Science teacher and lecturer.

Her background was all too typical of our day and age:

> From early childhood to the age of twenty, I was driven by a yearning for love. When I was five years old my parents were divorced. When my mother left our home never to return, I was raised by my father. We had a series of perhaps fifteen housekeepers who came and went until I was

twelve, and by that time I had been given most of the cooking and housework to do. Though my father did his best to care for my sister and me, his efforts were woefully inadequate. I became increasingly bitter and resented the absence of a mother to whom I could turn and confide my hopes for a career in the arts. My father understood nothing of this desire and did everything he could to discourage me.

When it was time for her to go to college, Deborah chose one far from home. She wrote seldom to her family, feeling little but hatred between them. In three years she was in a state of deep depression. Her life seemed broken up by an unhappy love affair; she was doing poorly in her academic work, drinking heavily, using several kinds of medication, and taking amphetamines and sleeping pills in increasing doses. Then came memory lapses and suicidal urges, a terrible loneliness, and a total lack of purpose. Finally, after a sleepless night, she saw only two choices before her: suicide or hard drugs.

At that time her chosen career was ballet, and she had often found the ballet studio a refuge. In her moment of desperation she went to the studio, hoping to find someone to comfort her. It was early and no one was there. In utter frustration she stood in the hall, crying bitterly. The director of the ballet company came out of her office to see what was wrong, invited her in, then asked what was troubling her. Out poured the sad story, and the director said quietly, "I think what you need is religion." Deborah, who had left her own church some years before, responded, "I don't need religion, I need some practical help." At that point the director pushed a copy of *Science and Health* across the desk and suggested that she might like to read it. Not wanting to offend her, Deborah took it, unimpressed:

> I was insulted by this offer of religion, which to me seemed a crutch for people too weak to stand on their own feet. In anger I walked down the street and into the nearest bar, slammed the book on the bar, and ordered a drink. As I stood there, it occurred to me I could help this woman by pointing out to her that religion, especially Christian Science, had no practical value. Then I thought, How can I do that when I don't know anything about Christian Science except that Christian Scientists "don't believe in doctors"? I decided to read the book as a source of some good ammunition.
>
> It didn't make much sense to me as I read, and much of it antagonized me, except for one phrase that contained the most beautiful words I had ever read: "Love supports the struggling heart until it ceases to sigh over the world and begins to unfold its wings for heaven."
>
> But this didn't alter my determination to refute Christian Science. I went to the ballet director's office several times a week to point out to her

the fallacies of Christian Science, asking questions in a spirit of bellig-erence, convinced that each question would knock the props out from under her religion. She answered each question satisfactorily, and her great love neutralized my venom. After several weeks I began to ask questions that had really been perplexing me and had not been answered by my previous religion: Who am I? What is my identity? Where am I going? As she patiently answered my questions, I felt a growing sense of purpose, a reason for being. My feelings of loneliness and fear began to abate.

Finally she had a healing of an injured hand. In her account she tells of "standing on the stairs, looking at my bleeding and bruised hand and thinking: Of course Christian Science doesn't work, but if it did work and I were a Christian Scientist, what would I do right now?" She decided then that if she were a Christian Scientist her course would be simple, since "Christian Science teaches that God is good and is all-presence, so all has to be good, and there is nothing outside of good." When she looked at her hand there wasn't a mark on it. She was awestruck before something she still couldn't understand. But, in her own words, "for the first time in my life I felt the presence of something greater than myself and knew that somehow I could learn to utilize this healing power."

One important passage of her life was now close to completion, as the next two paragraphs show, but only as the prelude to a new passage with new challenges and insights.

> Continuing to read *Science and Health*, I saw clearly that its author had compassion for mankind's yearnings and search for truth when she wrote: ". . . man, left to the hypotheses of material sense unexplained by Science, is as the wandering comet or the desolate star—'a weary searcher for a viewless home.'" . . . I began to see my life as immortal because it always was inseparable from God; in fact, God Himself was my life and I was His image and likeness. I now understood what Christ Jesus meant when he said, "Before Abraham was, I am," and what Paul meant when he said, "Your life is hid with Christ in God." With the realization of my eternal identity as a child of God, I rose in the dignity of man's immortal selfhood.
>
> By the time I had finished reading the book, I was a Christian Scientist. I couldn't remember the last time I had taken Speed. The need had left, and I was free. There were no struggles, no anxieties. As cynicism and bitterness dropped away, I was transformed. The Christian Scientist who had given me *Science and Health* had literally loved the hell out of me.

The next two selections represent two very different but complementary responses to mid-life crises or challenges. The first takes the form of a highly subjective poem, the second of a reasoned analysis.

The poem was written by a friend of mine during his late thirties when he was having a great inner struggle over whether he had sufficient spirituality and plain guts to give his whole life over to the healing work of Christian Science. It was, he told me, a period of agonizing self-doubt and desperate longing—an identity crisis in which he took a forlorn comfort from the Genesis story of Jacob's wrestling all night with the angel at Peniel. That struggle took on added meaning for him when he remembered Eddy's words: "The very circumstance, which your suffering sense deems wrathful and afflictive, Love can make an angel entertained unawares."[9] Still, the light didn't wholly break through. His own unworthiness seemed an insuperable block to what God was calling upon him to do.

At this point he remembered two lines from the poem "Carrion Comfort" by Gerard Manley Hopkins: "That night, that year / Of now done darkness I wretch lay wrestling with (my God!) my God." Reaching out to his bookshelves for the collected poems of that tortured and illumined priest-poet and turning to "Carrion Comfort," he read the opening lines:

> Not, I'll not, carrion comfort, despair, not feast on thee;
> Not untwist—slack they may be—these last strands of man
> In me or, most weary, cry *I can no more.* I can;
> Can something, hope, wish day come, not choose not to be. . . .[10]

The minimalism of those four lines reached my friend like the first faint light of dawn and he found himself thinking, "I *can*—at least I *can*." And having accepted that, he knew that he must do what Jacob did when the angel said to him, "Let me go, for the day breaketh," and Jacob replied, "I will not let thee go, except thou bless me." As my friend put it, he knew that he must learn every lesson and cherish every step in his passage toward the full light of day—the full blessing. The immediate result was a poem he wrote, frankly echoing some of Hopkins's own packed idiom and sprung rhythm:

> O Father Hopkins, that across chaos, a chasm, a creed deeplier
>   divisive than ocean or century,
> I thus should hear your speech ring with promise at the
>   reckless midnight of my private anguish.
> Ah well, indeed, God's grace is regardless; it falls like the
>   lightning, like the dew, too,
> Blasting and blessing, though we beat our foreheads at the
>   Bethel stone of our loneliness. You too
> Knew what I now know, dimly or dazzled by; were granted the
>   grace to somehow distinguish

The ladder that leads lightwise from I can to I am; the wrestle
that wrings hardlier the be from maybe.

Not choose—no more than first rung—*not to be*. But O that
    be, that all-but-unattainable wonder
Whose all-but harries the No of the faceless Foe with hope like
    the half-imagined morning faintness
That sweetens the east before we are sure, before mind shapes
    the coming crystal victory.
Still bruised by night, still unused to new light, I feel you,
    Father Hopkins, beside me benedictory
On this lowliest rung, clinging to least I can. But man, I
    must leave you anon, in fairness,
For full revelation, for stark and superb I Am, whose loveliest
    light now breaks on the world like thunder.

This was both a thank-you and a good-bye to a much-loved poet, for the
rest of my friend's life was unreservedly devoted to what he saw as the very
Science of Being—the "loveliest light" of the healing Christ.

The next account is taken from a talk given in 1960 as part of a radio and
television series on Christian Science healing experiences.[11] The speaker
told of his own rough journey to the acceptance of Christian Science. He
began by sharing his early frustration with the "real mess" that God (if there
was one!) had made of creation. Finding little satisfaction in religion, he
undertook an intensive study of the great philosophies, only to meet with
more frustration. Although he admired the rigorous logic of the various
philosophers, he soon found that in order to accept their conclusions one had
to accept their premises, which were "by definition just hypotheses." At no
point, he found, could one stop and say "this is it, this is the truth." So he
became an atheist and for ten years "thought and studied in that direction."
The speaker's wife had always been a Christian Scientist, and he had
"always argued with her about it." But he had also seen some good healings
through Christian Science take place in his own family. Finally he decided
there was "something there" that he greatly needed to understand, but the
path was still a rough one, as his further account made clear:

> Christian truths are beautiful in their simplicity, but I was still arguing
> on the side of matter. To me matter was substance and basis of all life. You
> see, I'd spent many years studying it, weighing it, measuring it, consider-
> ing its uses, limitations, handicaps. It seemed much more real to me than
> God, about whom I knew little or nothing.
> At first I couldn't accept Christian Science. I remember one day while

driving a farm tractor I was thinking about a statement in *Science and Health* (p. 468) where Mrs. Eddy writes: "There is no life, truth, intelligence, nor substance in matter. All is infinite Mind and its infinite manifestation, for God is All-in-all."

This seemed impossible to accept, when the sun was blazing down, the transmission case was burning my feet, a choking dust was boiling up from the plows, and the exhaust was roaring in my ears.

Then there was another thing that struck me as utterly impossible—the Bible statement that man is made in the image and likeness of God. How in the name of logic, I wondered, could each individual in the diverse multitude of humanity be the image and likeness of the one alone God?

The turning point came for the speaker when he was crippled with agonizing back pain (from a childhood injury that had caused him trouble ever since). He agreed to call a Christian Science practitioner, who came to the house.

One of the things [the practitioner] discussed was how very much God loved me. He spoke with such deep conviction that I found myself really believing that there was at least that possibility.

On about the second or third day, after a little nap, I woke up with a very warm sense of light. It was a wonderful inward glow of light and love. Apparently it was that my consciousness was opening up to the real presence and meaning of divine Love. But anyway, I knew right then that I was healed. And I was healed. Never again did I feel any pain from this back.

Actually, though, the physical healing wasn't the most important part of it. The really important thing to me was this. I now was satisfied there is a God, a very loving God, and that I could turn to Him again and again, in perfect trust, no matter what the problem might be.

I had to come to firm grips with this business of matter. I had to move my thinking over into an area where I could recognize God, divine Mind, as the starting point. I had to see that Spirit, God, is All, completely supreme, as Christian Science teaches. Therefore that matter is an illusion, or false concept, is actually unreal.

Steeped in materialism as I was, this was a long distance to travel. And it wasn't easy. But I could see that there isn't an experience we have that is outside of our thinking. To accept matter into our thinking as real is to surrender our thinking to material limitations, material impositions and laws. So to break away from material concepts is not only a perfectly intelligent but legitimate thing to do. It's not only the honest and good thing to do, but ultimately we are virtually forced to it because the propositions of matter lead to such an ultimate dissatisfaction that we just throw up our hands and give them up, recognize them as being utterly useless.

I saw that when we accept into our thinking the real import of God's infinitude, God's ever-presence—and consequently when I recognize that I am the expression of God's selfhood and have no other identity—this rules out materialistic thinking and the discords it imposes on the physical body. If man is made in the likeness of God, as the Bible says, then he can only express divine intelligence and wisdom—in fact all the spiritual qualities of God. In other words, the image of God must be a spiritual idea and not a mortal material being.

This was certainly a very new concept to me and there isn't a part of my life that hasn't been blessed. The pessimism and confusion disappeared. I was led into a useful and interesting career, as an electronic scientist doing systems engineering work for the Government.

The speaker ended his testimony by expressing his gratitude for having found a "completely satisfying answer" to his search for God.

From the hundreds of testimonies in which Christian Scientists tell how they have met the challenges and overcome the limitations of old age, I have chosen a very simple, undramatic one to illustrate this next-to-the-last passage of human existence. I say next-to-the-last passage because death is not regarded in Christian Science as the end of existence but rather as a transition to a new phase of experience on a new plane of consciousness.

This testimony was published in the *Christian Science Sentinel* of January 23, 1965, one year before the centennial commemoration of Eddy's "discovery" of Christian Science. The writer of the account was actually born three years before that historic event of the last century. The Pleasant View Home to which she refers was a retirement facility for veteran Christian Science practitioners and others who had given faithful service to the church. It stood on the site of the house in Concord, New Hampshire, where Eddy had spent sixteen years of her own amazingly active "retirement" before she returned for her last three years to Boston and the founding of the *Monitor.* With the appearance of locally run retirement and nursing homes for Christian Scientists all over the country, the centralized Pleasant View institution was finally closed as unnecessary.

The ultimate goal had been expressed in *Science and Health:* "Except for the error of measuring and limiting all that is good and beautiful, man would enjoy more than threescore years and ten and still maintain his vigor, freshness, and promise. . . . Let us then shape our views of existence into loveliness, freshness, and continuity, rather than into age and blight."[12]

The full realization of this vision lies a great distance ahead, but the unpretentious testimony of Mrs. Mina L. VanDam that follows—like the experience of many others in this century, both in and out of Christian Science—hints at the possibility:

According to the world's way of counting, I am now over one hundred and two years old. Christian Science found me when I was a young woman of twenty-three. I had been given up by the doctors, who said I had quick consumption. Each day I was wrapped up well and put on the porch.

One day a lady came by and asked me if I knew anything of Christian Science. I said I had heard of it, but knew nothing of its teachings. She brought me literature and talked to me. I accepted all she told me of God wholeheartedly.

I had no definite Christian Science treatment, but simply read a copy of *The Christian Science Journal*. I lived with that *Journal* for one month. After that time I walked out to the barn; then I went upstairs—a thing I had not [been able to do] for a long time. I obtained a copy of *Science and Health* by Mrs. Eddy. Within a year, much to the amazement of my neighbors and my husband, who later took up the study of Christian Science, I was completely well. I drove the horse and cut the lawn and was quite normal again.

Mrs. VanDam went on to say that for the past twelve years or so she had been living in the Christian Science Pleasant View Home in Concord. She also listed a few details of her life there. The "prayerful work" she speaks of is an in-house phrase denoting the metaphysical study and prayer that constitute Christian Science treatment.

I study the Lesson-Sermon from the *Quarterly* daily: I read all our periodicals regularly. I love *The Christian Science Monitor;* as I read it I do prayerful work for the world. Also I do prayerful work for our Home here. I enjoy walking up the broad corridor to the sun-room in the wintry weather. I like the out-of-doors.

I am more grateful than I can say for all the blessings that have come to me through the study of Christian Science; and for our Leader, Mrs. Eddy, my gratitude knows no bounds, because she unlocked the treasures of truth in the Bible for us all to know and use. [13]

This, of course, still leaves the ultimate mortality of earthly experience to be faced. As Paul says, "The last enemy that shall be destroyed is death"— destroyed, not sentimentalized as a friend or accepted as God's will for His creation. Christian Scientists take very seriously the words of Jesus: "If a man keep my saying, he shall never see death"—and they point to deathbed healings today that come close to the deathbed healings of the New Testament. But they also recognize that the full demonstration of immortality can be made only as every last vestige of sin is wiped from individual consciousness.

When Christian Scientists speak of death as unreal, they are not denying it as a physical phenomenon or a phase of human experience. But they are denying it as the supposed end of individual identity and being. To use a rough analogy, if one sees a mirage in a desert, something is certainly there; the question is whether it is an actual oasis or merely a delusive optical phenomenon. Is it *really* what it seems to be? One can ask the same question in regard to all the phases of material existence, including death.

Christian Science views death—or more exactly "the change called death"—as a passage, not a terminus, in one's journey toward true selfhood. Emily Dickinson might rightly say of death that "none may return to tell the tale of passage," but Eddy found in the resurrection and ascension of Jesus the supreme symbol and assurance of a continuing advance beyond the grave toward the eventual realization and actualization of what it means to live, move, and have one's being wholly in God, infinite Spirit. The Savior himself could say to Mary Magdalene, "I ascend unto my Father, *and your Father; and to my God, and your God*" (emphasis added).

What this may mean to a person heartbroken by the death of someone so deeply loved that life now seems hopelessly empty is suggested in a very simple way by a widely circulated little pamphlet first published more than sixty years ago.[14] It was based on the remembered conversation of two women friends sitting on the deck of an ocean liner. One, a Christian Scientist, had been trying to comfort the other, who earlier that year had had a shattering loss. The listener sat there quietly, grateful but unable to share her friend's warm assurance of the continuity of individual being. At the same time she idly watched the sea gulls playing around the mast of the ship as it plowed through the water:

> Presently she noticed that one of the gulls had left the others, circling higher and higher, until it was evident that it had separated itself from them altogether and was taking a course straight away from the ship. On and on it flew, steadily, surely, its strong white wings outspread, until it became a mere speck in the sky and finally was lost sight of altogether.
>
> But has the sea gull gone anywhere? thought the silent watcher, who was still pondering those comforting words she had just heard of the teaching of Christian Science regarding what is called death. Had that beautiful activity ceased? Was it not still identified with life, and strength, and vigor, and all that it possessed when it passed from her view? Had anything stopped? She suddenly sat up in her chair and gazed in almost startled interest at the blue far horizon, as into her consciousness there flowed an indescribable peace, the first she had known in many weary months. For she saw the truth of what her friend had been telling her and realized as never before that what had happened in her experience was just like the passing of the sea gull beyond her range of vision: it was still going on and on, even though her limited, human sense of sight could no longer follow it.

If I could see only a little farther, she thought. . . .

The rest of her account tells how her subsequent study of Christian Science enabled her to do just that.

To see a little farther into the great realities of being—and so to rise "clearer and nearer to the great heart of Christ"—is an aim any Christian may long to see realized. But we are greatly helped in our quest by the fellowship of other Christians. We are not, as members of the body of Christ, alone. Community of spirit is an important element in apprehending the continuity of being.

·8·

Church and Care

The First Church of Christ, Scientist, in Boston, Mass., is designed to be built on the Rock, Christ; even the understanding and demonstration of divine Truth, Life, and Love, healing and saving the world from sin and death; thus to reflect in some degree the Church Universal and Triumphant.

—Manual of The Mother Church

In Christian Science great emphasis is put on individual salvation, one's individual relation with God, one's individual responsibilities to one's fellow beings. It is often thought of as a highly individualistic form of religion, but this is largely a misunderstanding. Its emphasis is on individuality, not individualism. Eddy wrote, "I believe in no *ism*,"[1] and the statement holds true for other values she stressed: spirituality but not spiritualism, humanity but not humanism, intellectuality but not intellectualism, community but not communism.

Community, in the sense of a deeply shared spiritual purpose, mutual helpfulness, and wholehearted participation in the responsibilities and rewards of organized church activity, is the underlying theme of this chapter. It is another name for the normal fellowship of any group embarked on a thrilling but hazardous pilgrimage toward a common goal.

The Church of Christ, Scientist, was formed in 1879 "to reinstate primitive Christianity and its lost element of healing."[2] Later, as the movement began to spread to other countries, its founder reorganized the church into its present form, with a mother church in Boston and branch churches and societies around the world. The distribution of powers between the church in Boston and its branches is set forth in Eddy's *Manual of The Mother Church* and suggests in some ways the federal system of the United States, with the *Manual* as its Constitution.

While authority on basic policy is centered in The Mother Church, the branches are democratically self-governed within the broad structural framework established by the *Manual*. Most Christian Scientists are members of both their local branch church and The Mother Church. The first relates them especially to Christian Science activity within their own families and communities, the second to the movement's outreach to the needs of humankind as a whole.

From her earliest years Eddy had been, in her own words, "a child of the Church, an eager lover and student of vital Christianity,"[3] but by mid-life she had become disillusioned with ecclesiasticism as such. In the first edition of *Science and Health* in 1875 she wrote: "No time was lost by our Master in organization, rites, and ceremonies, or in proselyting for certain forms of belief: members of his church must answer to themselves, in the secret sanctuary of Soul, questions of the most solemn import."[4]

Experience with her early students, however, soon convinced her that so long as we live in a humanly organized society and need organic (that is, physically organized) bodies to express our present limited sense of individual identity, so long will the church as the collective body of Christ need organized or institutional expression and thus reflect "in some degree"[5] the wholly spiritual Church Universal and Triumphant.

In an address at the laying of the cornerstone of The First Church of Christ, Scientist, in Boston in 1894 she expressed this unusual concept in a typical blend of the practical and the ideal:

> To-day I pray that divine Love, the life-giving Principle of Christianity, shall speedily wake the long night of materialism, and the universal dawn shall break upon the spire of this temple. The Church, more than any other institution, at present is the cement of society, and it should be the bulwark of civil and religious liberty. But the time cometh when the religious element, or Church of Christ, shall exist alone in the affections, and need no organization to express it. Till then, this form of godliness seems as requisite to manifest its spirit, as individuality to express Soul and substance.[6]

Meanwhile her aim was to keep the organization as simple and supple as possible. She was well aware that any institution formed for a worthy, unselfish purpose ran the risk of finally losing sight of the purpose and becoming an end in itself. On the other hand she recognized the danger of an antinomian spirit that resisted the disciplines and thereby the rewards of genuine Christian community. One of the officers of The Mother Church recorded a conversation he had with her on this subject a year before her death:

> She spoke of the Christian Scientists who go about saying we need no organization as "not knowing what they are talking about." She also said, in substance, "Organization is a simple matter, for all of its importance. It is simply a matter of doing things by working together."[7]

The *Manual* as left by Eddy is no ponderous body of canon law covering every detail of church policy and procedure. A small book of rules and bylaws, completed in 1910, it sets forth once and for all the basic the church. It is both a practical handbook and a spiritual members of a church of laypersons, a church without clergy, anything that can be properly called rites or ceremonies. An be elected or appointed to any office in the church, if he or s have the requisite spiritual, moral, intellectual, and practica for its duties—an ideal in which spiritual demonstration must more than academic education or worldly skills. In addition, li service are normal in all elective offices, and Mother Church a prerequisite for holding certain branch church positions.

It may be useful to note parenthetically that many of the m figures in Christian Science history—for example, Edward John M. Tutt, Julia M. Johnston—held no executive positions in based organization. Their wide influence in the movement came their work as practitioners, teachers, writers, and speakers, a ro that of a pastoral counselor or a seminary professor than of a churc an archbishop.

The *Manual* provides that the only "preaching" at Christi Sunday services shall be a "lesson-sermon" composed of select from the Bible and *Science and Health* on a given topic. This is congregation by a First and Second Reader chosen by the chu members to serve for a three-year term. As a "lesson," these re have already been studied daily in the preceding week by most of the members. But as a "sermon" it is now being listened to as a shared experience, and many are praying that its inspiration and healing power may reach all those present—and indeed flow out to the whole community.

In a way, such prayer is a test of the genuine Christianity of a church's members. Over the years, I have occasionally heard members of other denominations say that when they visited a Christian Science Sunday service out of curiosity they found it cold, formal, and uninspiring. Others visiting for the first time have told me they felt the exact opposite: a sense of quietude and spiritual attentiveness, but also of encompassing love. These contrasting responses may be explained as differences in the degree of spiritual inspiration and commitment expressed in the particular service visited—or of spiritual hunger and receptivity in the respective visitors. In her *Message to The Mother Church for 1901*, Eddy, after a disquisition on God as both infinite Person and infinite Principle, commented on those who objected to the Christian Science form of service as too impersonal:

> True, I have made the Bible, and "Science and Health with Key to the Scriptures," the pastor for all the churches of the Christian Science denomination, but that does not make it impossible for this pastor of ours to preach! . . . The Word of God is a powerful preacher, and it is not too spiritual to be practical, nor too transcendental to be heard and understood. Whosoever saith there is no sermon without personal preaching, forgets what Christian Scientists do not, namely, that God is a Person, and that he should be willing to hear a sermon from his personal God![8]

A 1984 editorial in the *Christian Science Journal* quotes this passage and goes on to comment:

> Obviously, she expected her pastor to preach to the congregation—that is, to inspire and to transform the lives of the listeners. And it does, if the hearers are awake and really listening.
>
> For example, a short time after the Bible and *Science and Health* had been ordained as pastor of The Mother Church, a man named Henry Eaton, who had been badly injured in an accident and been treated by fourteen or fifteen different doctors without success, asked for Christian Science treatment. He was treated for about a year, and there was enough improvement so he could get out to the service at The Mother Church.
>
> He said that when he first attended, his head almost touched the pew in front of him, but the church, the people, the music, and the lesson all helped him see that God is Love. He continued to have Christian Science treatment and to attend services. After two years he was healed of the original injury and all the deformity and suffering associated with it. You can feel the joy and the strong, new sense of life in his article called "Free Indeed," published in the July 1898 *Journal*.[9]

The functions of the church, as spelled out in the *Manual*, may be subsumed under three headings: worship, education, and spiritual fellowship. The activities in these three categories frequently overlap, as illustrated by the weekly lesson-sermons and also by the midweek testimony meetings, in which spontaneous accounts of healing, guidance, and regeneration given by members of the congregation are preceded by a "lesson" prepared by the First Reader—that is, readings from the Bible and *Science and Health* on a topic he or she has chosen as appropriate to meet the current needs and thinking of the members.

In addition to daily individual prayer and study, educational activities are provided by the *Manual:* Sunday Schools for pupils up to the age of twenty, a short, intensive course of instruction by authorized teachers for those wishing a solid spiritual grounding in the metaphysics and practice of Christian Science, a course for training selected practitioners to teach such classes, public lectures on Christian Science by the members of a board of lectureship drawn from experienced practitioners especially suitable for such a mission, and the weekly, monthly, and quarterly denominational publications, which help to relate the basic spiritual teachings of the church to the evolving trends of the general culture.

Reading rooms, often located in crowded shopping and business districts, are intended to serve as quiet havens for reading, study, and prayer. Christian Science organizations at universities and colleges serve the special needs of Christian Scientists in academic communities and are augmented by occasional international conferences in Boston to which thousands of students and faculty members come from all parts of the world. In past years an arrangement between The Mother Church and Boston University has permitted qualified young Christian Scientists who wish to serve as Protestant chaplains in the Armed Services of the United States to receive the necessary background training at the university's School of Theology.

During this same period there have been various encouraging expressions of ecumenicity and dialogue with mainline churches. These range from lectures on Christian Science at the Ecumenical Institute in Bossey, Switzerland, and attendance as guests at World Council of Churches conferences, to active participation in local councils of churches and ministerial associations in a number of communities.

Although hardly to be classified as a social activist church, the Christian Science denomination harbors many social activists among its adherents, and the *Christian Science Monitor* strives to foster social awareness and concern in its readers.[10] The church has a tradition of generous giving to philanthropies and of large-scale participation in disaster and war relief activities.[11] Ministries to prisoners have been carried on since early in the church's history. Most branch churches have care committees to look into the needs of lonely, ailing, or incapacitated members, and some of them extend this practical concern to needy individuals and families in the neighborhood or the community at large.

As from the beginning, however, Christian Scientists regard spiritual healing as their chief contribution to society. By this I do not mean the healing of disease only, but also of the whole range of evils built into the nature and limitations of mortal existence. If this sounds grandiose, the following illustration will cut it down to a meaningful size.

Some years ago I spoke with a Christian Science practitioner who was chosen by her branch church to represent it in the local ministerial association. She told me that for the first few meetings with these mainline pastors she wondered just why she was there. Most of the issues they discussed seemed peripheral to her own concerns and those of her local church. But suddenly she saw the light: she was a practitioner and her work was to *heal*. And something in the group obviously needed healing. It was clear from their discussion that for all their goodwill the strong cleavage between the liberals and conservatives among them often made agreement very difficult.

She began to pray silently at such times, turning in confidence to God as the one ever-present, infinite Mind governing and coordinating all the elements of its spiritual universe in perfect harmony and mutual understanding. On several occasions her prayer led her to suggest a practical solution which resulted in reconciling two seemingly intractable positions, much to the joy of all concerned. At other times, as she prayed, the heat of argument would suddenly abate and a rational compromise be reached with surprising ease. As time went on, she felt a growing affection for these men of God (she was the only woman member, as I recall). In turn, they recognized the healing quality of her participation by electing her as their chairperson for the coming year—despite the fact that she had been admitted only as a nonvoting member!

Christian Scientists often think of their healing prayers for others as a leaven at work in human thought, unknown to the world in general, and they take pleasure in Jesus' words: "The kingdom of heaven is like unto leaven, which a woman took, and hid in three measures of meal, till the whole was leavened" (Matthew 13:33). Eddy interpreted the three measures of meal as standing for science, theology, and medicine, all to be transformed in time by the Holy Spirit understood as a divine science. For the purpose of this book, the "health and medicine" aspect of the church's "caring" activity is of first importance.

The healing function of a Christian Science practitioner has already been described in Chapter 5. The work of a Christian Science nurse is to take care of the practical needs of a sick or disabled person while the practitioner carries on the actual spiritual healing. The two roles are complementary. The nurse, too, needs to pray—not directly for the patient, but to maintain a mental atmosphere that supports the patient's own spiritual endeavors. As

Science and Health puts it, "The nurse should be cheerful, orderly, punctual, patient, full of faith,—receptive to Truth and Love."[12] A writer for the *Christian Science Sentinel* commented wryly after quoting this sentence that one might be tempted to exclaim—like the small Boy Scout when he was read the list of qualities expected of a scout—"All at *once?*" Christian Science nursing surely requires spiritual dedication as well as professional skill.

The *Manual* provides for such nurses but says nothing about their training. Eddy did, however, express to her church officers the importance of such training. Under the system that has developed, a Christian Science graduate nurse must complete a three-year course of training. The academic portion of this course is given at four nurses' training schools accredited by The Mother Church and located at Boston, San Francisco, London (England), and Princeton (New Jersey).[13] On-the-job training is given at a number of Christian Science sanatoriums, which are recognized in the United States under the federal Medicare program and also by leading insurance companies, as providing acceptable "hospitalization" for those needing Christian Science nursing care.[14] The nurses' training is entirely nonmedical, but includes, among other subjects, classes in basic nursing arts (for example, feeding, bathing, applying dressings, and bandaging), care of the elderly, cookery for invalids, nursing ethics, obstetric theory, and care of reportable diseases—but no medication or physical therapy of any kind.

Over the years a number of medical nurses who have become Christian Scientists have chosen to switch over to Christian Science nursing, but they too must go through part of the training program so that they can understand clearly the different function and focus of the new vocation. The first requirement of a Christian Science nurse in the *Manual* is that he or she shall be one "who has a demonstrable knowledge of Christian Science practice," and only then comes the stipulation that he or she shall also be one "who thoroughly understands the practical wisdom necessary in a sick room, and who can take proper care of the sick."[15]

The practitioner's work is to cure, the nurse's simply to care for the patient's temporary needs. Yet the two are closely related, and a nurse's earnest prayer to keep her own thought clear can certainly help to provide a mental atmosphere conducive to healing.

In general, Christian Science nurses at the present time tend to prefer working in a sanatorium or other care facility to taking on the less structured but more demanding role of a privately employed or visiting nurse who cares for patients in their own homes. Both kinds of service are in heavy demand, but the last-named accords more closely with Eddy's concept of nursing as a religious vocation as well as a profession. The institutionalizing of Christian

Science nursing undoubtedly meets a present need, but it points to a larger problem facing the Church of Christ, Scientist.

Eddy wished to safeguard the church's radically spiritual purpose from the proliferation of subsidiary social organizations and activities that she felt were draining from liberal Protestantism the pure, redemptive spirituality at the heart of Christianity. This viewpoint is summed up in an ecumenical position paper published by the church in 1969:

> The Saviour's healing of the leper and the cripple was not irrelevant to the larger needs of a leprous and crippled society. . . . If the Church allows itself to become only one more welfare or reform organization among many, then it stands to lose its unique power and may well end up committed to a program of stifling social coercion rather than of liberating social redemption—to the ethics of the ant-heap rather than of the Kingdom.
>
> Surely the Church has a continuing commitment to awaken in its members that blazing sense of spiritual power, reality, and love which *heals*. And does this not properly begin with the healing of the Christian's own alienation from his divine source? Individual redemption remains a vital wellspring of genuine social therapy. [16]

In this perspective, even such activities as Christian Science sanatoriums and nursing or retirement homes can be regarded as temporary aids. They would presumably not be needed if the healing work of Christian Scientists was consistently at the level attributed to Jesus and the Apostles. Not being included in the *Manual*, these institutions may be considered as culturally a part of the Christian Science movement but not as organs of the Christian Science church. At the same time, they are recognized and given occasional advice by The Mother Church if they measure up to the standards set by both the state and the church.

Eddy encouraged the support of philanthropic and humanitarian projects of many kinds. [17] On one occasion she even sent a generous financial contribution to the Newton Hospital near her home, possibly to show her appreciation of the indispensable service such institutions provide for the vast majority of people who rely on medicine for healing. Nevertheless she saw that some members of her own church would become so fascinated by the machinery of caring for the human needs of those seeking help in Christian Science that they would lose sight of its basic mission to heal "the sins of the world."

The same is true of other organizations of varying worth which have sprung up over the years with an ambiguous relationship to The Mother Church. The list includes private schools and camps for young Christian Scientists, [18] independent foundations to promote Christian Science in one way or another,[19] Christian Science businessmen's luncheon clubs,[20] historical societies,[21] and off-beat publishing ventures.[22] Opinions vary greatly as to the usefulness and legitimacy of these activities, but the fact that the *Manual* makes no provision for them means that The Mother Church can take no official responsibility for them, and they must therefore stand or fall on their own merits.

In the light of these considerations, a one-sentence dictum by Eddy in 1904 becomes less cryptic: "Good deeds overdone numerically, or bad deeds, are remedied by reading the Manual."[23] In a letter to a male student who was bursting with a new scheme to promote Christian Science, she wrote in the same year: "Your letter is characteristic, wit and adventure smile together, [they] promise but decoy. Your many students and followers speak well for you. But dear one, if the plan you suggest were wise it would have had its birth in The Mother Church Manual, that is the law of our Gospel—and born of necessity to guide the children of Christian Science."[24]

Again in the same year, when she was giving special attention to the permanence of the *Manual*, she inserted a new bylaw which in its final, revised form read that members of The Mother Church should not "unite with organizations which impede their progress in Christian Science."[25] Obviously, Christian Scientists belong to a variety of secular organizations. For the most part this gives them a further opportunity to put their Christianity into practice, as in the already cited case of the practitioner in the ministerial association. But at other times a clear choice between expediency and principle may be called for in deciding whether to join an organization that would compromise one's standards and convictions as a Christian Scientist.

The experience of a close friend in a country behind the Iron Curtain provides a good example. Because he was doing important research in chemistry he was given a favored position by the Communist government. But eventually he was told that he must join a certain organization that would involve some degree of ideological commitment to the political system. Failure to join would bring severe limitations on the freedom of his family and himself. Some of his Christian Scientist friends advised him to join, since the Communist commitment would be merely nominal. Others urged him as a Christian Scientist to take his stand on Principle and be ready to suffer the consequences.

But he didn't want mere human opinion. As a Christian Scientist he believed in the reign of divine law, and suddenly he felt that somewhere in the bylaws of the *Manual* he would find the scientific answer to his dilemma.

When he came to the bylaw about not joining organizations that would impede his progress in Christian Science, he found his answer. He could not and would not join, but since he was under the protection of divine law he need suffer no penalty. Three times he received a notice telling him he had to join, but he simply gave no answer, assured that God's law was at work in the situation. And that was the end of it. More than thirty years have passed without penalty or comment from the authorities, and the liberties granted my friend and his family have increased rather than lessened.

To some disaffected Christian Scientists the *Manual of The Mother Church* seems a dated instrument putting arbitrary constraints on the individual and group actions of its members. To most Christian Scientists—as in the example just given—it seems an inspired instrument of liberation from the constrictions and clashes of unregenerate human wills. What is evident is that it has done more to hold Christian Scientists together as a religious community during the past hundred years than anything else except the two books it names as perpetual pastor of the Church of Christ, Scientist: the Holy Bible and *Science and Health with Key to the Scriptures.*

·9·

Spiritual Healing

Heal me, O Lord, and I shall be healed.
—Jeremiah 17:14

For the past forty years interest in spiritual healing has grown in mainline churches throughout the U.S. and in other countries. The number of books and articles on the subject has increased greatly in recent years. Yet the churches' support of this trend still shows a certain wariness.

In my book *Spiritual Healing in a Scientific Age* (1987), I suggested that this coolness may result from the traditional churches' fear that so fervent a movement could easily overstep the mark, claim too much, venture too far, and get into serious trouble by contesting the established authority of science in the care and cure of the body.[1] In the four years since I first drafted that statement, interest in the subject both within and beyond the churches has grown visibly stronger. However, the catholicity of the movement is not matched by unity of doctrine or practice. Charismatics, Pentecostalists, New Age mentalists, televangelists, quiet little evangelical prayer groups, devoted Christian doctors and hospital chaplains, antimedical fundamentalist faith healers, High Church Anglican priests healing through sacramental rites—these are only a few of the groups and individuals involved. The differences between these various approaches are so great that perhaps what is going on is better described as a tendency than as a movement.

Christian Scientists have welcomed this upsurge of active dedication to an element of Christianity so close to their own hearts. But they recognize that the radical spirituality of their metaphysical position, with the ontological unreality of matter as its corollary, still puts them in a unique position. There are frequently beautiful breakthroughs of understanding between individual Christian Scientists and Christian healers of other kinds, as well as a growing awareness of a common spirit to be found in differing approaches to the healing ministry. On this basis we may build a closer fellowship. But at the present time Christian Scientists are the only group whose convictions demand a totally new view of reality. Consequently more conservative spiritual healers, regarding Christian Science as an embarrassment rather than an ally, are apt to avoid contact with it altogether.

This last attitude is understandable insofar as the very term *Christian Science* suggests a bold encroachment on both the religion of the past and the science of the present. It is not quite so understandable when viewed in the light of the remarkable record of Christian Science healing in the last one hundred and twenty years.

More than 50,000 testimonies of healing have been published in the Christian Science periodicals during that time. Some of them recount in detail a single outstanding healing; many of them report a number of healings experienced by the testifiers and their families over a period of years— healings of ills, accidents, and crippling life situations of all sorts. A great many of the healings of serious disease have a previous history of medical treatment, hospitalization, repeated operations, and grim diagnoses and prognoses; some healings have actually taken place under medical observation. Other testimonies of a more anecdotal nature are attested by witnesses familiar with the situations described or with the character of the testifier.

This core material is preserved in the bound volumes of the *Christian Science Journal*, the *Christian Science Sentinel*, and the various foreign-language editions of the *Herald of Christian Science*. All these periodicals are available in most Christian Science Reading Rooms and some university and public libraries. It is augmented in Christian Science literature by innumerable other accounts of healing, presented as examples in various forms and contexts in articles, pamphlets, lectures, newspaper and magazine interviews, and radio and television programs—not to mention the spontaneous oral testimonies given at the eight million Wednesday evening meetings conservatively estimated to have been held in worldwide Christian Science churches in the past century.[2] Among the books dealing with various aspects of Christian Science are several focused specifically on the *kinds* of evidence offered in support of its healing claims. These include further detailed and documented accounts, some of them attested by physicians familiar with the cases.[3]

The first of these, by Benjamin O. Flower, editor of a mildly radical magazine, *The Arena*, was written in 1909 in answer to an article by a prominent Boston physician and professor at the Harvard Medical School, Richard C. Cabot. The latter, in his article "One Hundred Christian Science

Cures," had come to the conclusion that "most Christian Science cures are probably genuine" but "they are not cures of organic disease." Flower answered with detailed evidence from several reputable doctors and surgeons who had been convinced by their own experience that Christian Science definitely *did* cure organic and even terminal disease. (In those days the medical world made what is now regarded as a naive distinction between "organic" and "functional" disease.) He even included an account from the July 27, 1907, issue of the *Journal of the American Medical Association* of what was believed to be "the first instance recorded of recovery from generalized blastomycosis"—an account which left mysteriously unclear the circumstances of the patient's sudden recovery after two years of painful and unsuccessful medical treatment. Flower was able to put the somewhat elliptical case history from the medical journal alongside the detailed written account by the patient's husband of the startling change that began the day the last physician was dismissed and a Christian Science practitioner was called upon for treatment.

But this is ancient history, and as such cuts no ice with the present-day critic—although it appears to have made some impression on Dr. Cabot, who seventeen years after his denial that Christian Science could cure organic disease was quoted in the Harvard Alumni Bulletin of December 1, 1925, as saying: "I see no reason why we should admit only one of the different ways through which healing comes to our bodies. I want to take them all, and in that I disagree with Christian Science, the good effects of which I see on all sides. I have not the slightest doubt that it does good, that it cures disease, *organic as well as functional,* only I do not want anybody to say, 'And nothing else cures'" (emphasis added).

In the intervening years, however, a growing number of doctors have expressed privately if not publicly their conviction that Christian Science does heal many apparently hopeless cases. I have personally talked with quite a few who are very frank about this, and I have included several examples in my 1987 book on spiritual healing. A different kind of evidence occurs in a 1963 doctoral dissertation by Lee Zeunert Johnson:

> Some evidence also suggests that to the medical profession a factor tending to make the Church's position less radical has simply been the practical success of Christian Science healing. Twice on the radio programs of the Church from 1958 to 1960, a church member stated that a doctor had recommended Christian Science (program #273, healing of tuberculosis of an arm bone, as reported in the *Christian Science Sentinel*, LX [December 13, 1958], p. 2188; program #283, healing of fibroid tumor, *Sentinel*, LXI [February 21, 1959], p. 336). One testifier was guided by a doctor's wife

(program #250, healing of typhoid fever, *Sentinel*, LX [July 5, 1958], p. 1165). According to mimeographed *Reports on Fruitage From "How Christian Science Heals" Radio and Television Programs* (Boston: Committee on Publication)—an Alabama physician referred a patient to a Christian Science practitioner (March 1957 report), an Ohio doctor himself turned to Christian Science (September 1957), a Texas doctor and a Connecticut doctor supplied Christian Science literature to patients (April 1957 and November 1958 reports, respectively). It is noteworthy that, according to the *Monitor*'s editor, "the largest single professional group subscribing to the *Monitor*, as far as the paper's admittedly limited statistics on this point shed light, is the physicians." *Commitment to Freedom* [by Erwin D. Canham, 1958], p. 123.[4]

So far there has been little serious effort to make an objective medical assessment of the evidence available. There are, of course, inherent difficulties in measuring the effectiveness of spiritual healing with scientific precision. This has been aptly stated by a Quaker writer on the subject:

> We are confined almost exclusively to the historical method . . . since the higher spiritual forces do not lend themselves to normal scientific treatment; we cannot lay on faith, love, and holiness in a laboratory, to be used as desired, in the same way that we can provide water, electricity, and sulphuretted hydrogen. We can usually only investigate events that have already happened, with all the uncertainty that such historical methods imply.[5]

On the face of it, this would disqualify spiritual healing from scientific investigation or even recognition. A British medical historian refers to faith healing (as he calls it) as "a dangerous field placed between theology and medicine, that no one has dared thoroughly to explore."[6] Rex Gardner, a distinguished British physician who is also an ardent proponent of spiritual healing, adds that the risk any scholar runs in writing seriously on this subject is that of "academic suicide."[7] Elsewhere Gardner points out the tendency of his profession to dismiss even the most carefully documented case history of a "miraculous" healing as merely "anecdotal" evidence. He goes on to explain sardonically for the benefit of readers outside his profession that *anecdotal* is the "derisory adjective applied to any case-history that is used to support an argument with which the listener does not agree."[8]

In his book *Healing Miracles* Gardner gives a number of detailed case histories that he himself has observed or which have been reported to him by medical colleagues sympathetic to the possibilities of healing through prayer. In this he has an advantage over Christian Scientists reporting healings they have had when they turned to Christian Science after extensive hospitalization and medical treatment, sometimes in a terminal situation. Often the doctors who have seen such healings have said to them afterward, "This is a miracle!" or "Only God could have done this," or even "Stick with Christian Science if it can do things like this." But, understandably, few doctors are rash enough to put such statements into writing. Sometimes they agree to endorse the accuracy of an account of healing that a Christian Scientist wishes to send to the Christian Science periodicals for publication, but almost always a doctor will agree to this only after receiving written assurance that his or her name will not be made public. As Rex Gardner recognizes, even to grant the possibility of a "miracle" is to risk one's professional standing, though he himself and some of his colleagues have been gallantly willing to take that risk.

One of the case histories in his book concerns an eleven-month-old baby who after three months of progressive deterioration under expert and devoted medical care was discharged from the hospital as a hopeless case. A little later the child was taken by his parents to a Pentecostal healing service, and a few days after that he showed signs of improvement. From that time on, there was "steady, consistent progress" until he became a normal, healthy little boy.

Gardner quotes from the technical summary of the case as recorded by the doctor who treated the child in the hospital:

> He was treated initially with antibiotics to which there was no response and a definitive diagnosis of advancing fibrosing alveolitis was established by lung biopsy. He was treated for six weeks on high dosage corticosteroids without improvement, and for a further six weeks on corticosteroids combined with azathioprine, again without improvement. Blood-gas analyses over this period of three months showed progressive deterioration.

In completing the history, Gardner makes a point that is relevant to many other kinds of healing by prayer, including Christian Science:

> The professorial summary [by the doctor who treated the child] concludes: "The prognosis of fibrosing alveolitis starting in the first year of life is almost uniformly fatal." As already noted it is the word "almost" which makes proof of miraculous healing very difficult. However it would require a considerable degree of scepticism to believe that this was a rare case of spontaneous remission, which happened by sheer coincidence at exactly the same time as a healing service. When additionally the other Case Records [in Gardner's book] are considered, the likelihood of all these

cures being associated by mere chance with believing prayer must be astronomically remote.[9]

A Christian Scientist can read Gardner's book with warm appreciation of his honesty, courage, wit, compassion, and deep spiritual commitment to the healing imperative of biblical Christianity as he understands it—with the added fillip of his being a physician. But the book also serves to illustrate the theological and metaphysical differences between Christian Science and the large number of Christian healers who see their work as supplementary and complementary to orthodox medicine.

The general assumption behind this latter viewpoint is that the creator of our complex universe in his infinite but inscrutable wisdom may choose, most of the time, to cure disease through humanity's painfully acquired knowledge and skill in utilizing or manipulating the laws of nature as they are understood at any given time. But, the argument goes, this same omnipotent Deity may from time to time and for reasons unknown to us choose to intervene in a particular situation and bring healing through direct action in a way wholly inexplicable in terms of today's "scientific" medicine.

According to Gardner and his fellow believers, such healings are rightly called miracles, and a miracle can be neither predicted, demanded, nor guaranteed. But deep, humble prayer that God's will be done, they explain, opens the way for this kind of healing to come when it *is* God's will. Even if the prayer doesn't result in physical healing it may bring wonderful comfort, moral strengthening, and spiritual regeneration to the sufferer.

This is what might be called the classic form of Christian healing, as portrayed by such highly respected early historians of the movement as Evelyn Frost and Morton T. Kelsey and illustrated by such impressive healers as Agnes Sanford, Francis MacNutt, and Emily Gardner Neal. There are differences among them, but not crucial ones. They all go back to the New Testament and the early church fathers for their authority. Many of them in their healing work rely in varying degrees on such traditional practices as the laying on of hands, anointing with oil, the use of holy water, the administration of the sacraments, and the rites of exorcism. Virtually all of them see no conflict in working together with modern medicine and psychology—or, as one of them put it, bringing prayer together with medical and psychological models.

Even among the "classic" spiritual healers, however, there are those who balk a little at using the word *miracle* to describe even the most remarkable healings that take place as the result of prayer alone. Many of them are groping toward the concept of spiritual law rather than divine whim as governing such healings. This concept logically leads to questioning the ultimate adequacy of physical and biochemical explanations of disease. Yet, even so, it is hard for most of them to conceive the possibility of an actual science of Spirit that would rule out material causation as a mental misconception of how God works.

This is a more-than-quantum leap for the human mind to take, for nothing seems harder even for Christian believers to accept than the possibility that the kingdom of God is indeed an entirely different order of reality, demanding an entirely different kind of thinking in order to be realized as a demonstrable fact in present experience. To many good Christians it may still seem almost blasphemous to describe Jesus of Nazareth as "the most scientific man that ever trod the globe," with the explanation that he "plunged beneath the material surface of things and found the spiritual cause."[10] And to many it may be even more disturbing to be told that the Holy Spirit—the Comforter or Advocate which Jesus prophesied would guide his followers "into all truth"—should be thought of as an eternal, divine Science, predating and embracing all particular revelations.[11]

This helps to explain two related contemporary facts: (1) the uneasiness that keeps some Christian healers from feeling the fellowship with Christian Science that might be expected on grounds of common interest, and (2) the evidence that Christian Science and medicine, starting from opposite premises, do not ordinarily combine well in actual practice.

The first section of Chapter 5 has already touched on the latter point. However, the radical difference between the two approaches doesn't exclude the possibility of very cordial relations between Christian Science practitioners and physicians or public health officials when their paths converge on such matters as compulsory immunization, the reporting of diseases suspected of being contagious, obstetric cases like those mentioned in Chapter 7, or accidents in which a Christian Scientist may be rushed willy-nilly to a hospital but asks to be allowed to rely wholly on Christian Science treatment.[12]

Throughout its history, Christian Science has won some doctors to its ranks through striking healings they have either experienced or witnessed. Some have tried to combine their new faith with their medical practice but have usually found that for their own peace of mind they have eventually had to decide definitely for one way or the other. Among those who have chosen to go ahead actively with Christian Science, quite a few have become Christian Science practitioners. Some have ended by serving additionally as Christian Science teachers, lecturers, writers for the church periodicals, or church officers.[13]

In no way are Christian Scientists "against doctors." It is not unusual for testifiers who have turned to Christian Science and received a remarkable healing after a prior period of hospitalization and unsuccessful medical treatment to express very warm gratitude for the humanity and kindness shown to them by doctors and nurses while they were under their care. In a world full of suffering, it is obvious that the vast majority of people are not yet ready to put their entire trust in spiritual healing, and no one with a grain of sense can be anything but grateful to those who are unselfishly trying by whatever means possible to alleviate that suffering. What encourages Christian Scientists is the growing concern in the medical profession itself not to allow the new technologies of biomedicine and genetic manipulation to wipe out the perception of the individual as something much more than a physical or psychological mechanism.

Almost a century ago, Eddy—who herself had very warm and friendly relations with several doctors—wrote, "It is just to say that generally the cultured class of medical practitioners are grand men and women, therefore they are more scientific than are false claimants to Christian Science." And elsewhere in *Science and Health* she wrote, "If ecclesiastical sects or medical schools turn a deaf ear to the teachings of Christian Science, then part from these opponents as did Abraham when he parted from Lot, and say in thy heart: 'Let there be no strife, I pray thee, between me and thee, and between my herdmen and thy herdmen; for we be brethren.' "[14] Even more explicitly she wrote, "A genuine Christian Scientist loves Protestant and Catholic, D.D. and M.D.,—loves all who love God, good; and he loves his enemies." Also a bylaw in the *Manual* states flatly: "A member of this Church shall not publish, nor cause to be published, an article that is uncharitable or impertinent towards religion, medicine, the courts, or the laws of our land."[15]

HUMAN AND DIVINE LAW

The last twenty years of Eddy's life (1891–1910), when Christian Science was growing by leaps and bounds, were roughly the same period marked by the founding of Johns Hopkins Medical School at one end (1893) and the Flexner Report at the other (1910)—years when American medicine was being professionalized and the American Medical Association, as part of its war on irregular medical sects, was crusading vigorously for the suppression of Christian Science. This situation is summed up with unusual balance and fresh documentation in a 1986 *Medical Heritage* article by Thomas C. Johnsen, a Christian Scientist writer with a Johns Hopkins doctorate in history.[16] The article also serves incidentally to illustrate the kind of objective Christian Science scholarship that has sprung up in the past thirty years.

The early attacks on Christian Science healing were carried on in the courts, the legislatures, and the press, and in all three arenas Christian Science gradually established its legitimacy. One interesting point brought out by Johnsen is that the church's defense rested ultimately not on the argument for religious rights but on the pragmatic argument of successful healing.[17] There was widespread recognition by 1910 that it would be absurd to compel Christian Science practitioners to conform to the training and licensing requirements set by state medical boards for conventional physicians. Even Mark Twain, who had a healthy respect for Christian Science healing although at the same time he savaged its venerated leader and her church officials, made the mordant comment in 1903 that "if the Second Advent should happen now, Jesus could not heal the sick in the State of New York" under the medical practice acts then being proposed.[18]

The Second Advent meant to Christian Scientists not the return of the personal Jesus but of the Christ-power and the Christ-spirit that had been so supremely expressed in his life and works. Once again, they felt, that power and that spirit were being put on trial by human law. "Trials are proofs of God's care,"[19] Eddy had written, and the Christian Scientists at the beginning of this century seem to have been invigorated rather than depressed by the court cases and legislative challenges they faced. In the wake of the cases brought against Christian Science under medical licensing laws, Johnsen's article points out, more and more states "incorporated explicit 'saving' clauses into their codes affirming the legality of the practice of spiritual healing." And what that meant to the thinkers in the movement is suggested by the same article:

> From the Christian Scientists' standpoint, such recognition was a matter of equitable treatment under the law, not of preferential legislation. As former Iowa Judge Clifford Smith explained in 1914, in *Christian Science: Its Legal Status,* they did not seek any "special privilege" or legal establishment of religion, but solely to preserve rights threatened by efforts to prohibit their system of healing. The Smith book, probably the denomination's most thorough articulation of its position, was subtitled *A Defense of Human Rights;* the fact that the subtitle did not include the term "religious rights" was significant, since Christian Scientists saw the issue under consideration as far more than a narrow Constitutional question, or even than merely one of religious freedom. Judge Smith acknowledged, in any case, that such freedom is not absolute, and that it involves not only rights but also responsibilities—what Christian Scientists could properly expect from society and what society could reasonably demand from them. . . .

In 1901 Eddy herself issued a statement instructing church members to diligently obey legal requirements on vaccination and reporting of suspected contagious conditions—citing Jesus' injunction to "render unto Caesar what is Caesar's." While the JAMA [*Journal of the American Medical Association*] pronounced this statement an implicit "confession" of the failure of Christian Science, her student Alfred Farlow [first manager of the Christian Science Committee on Publication] pointed out that it was consistent with the broad emphasis of her teaching of respect for the rights of others: "I readily concede that Christian Scientists must not attempt to set aside the laws which stand for the general good of any community." Farlow admitted that "there may be unwise and careless Christian Scientists, who do and say unwise things," but insisted that "such people would be unwise and careless" whatever church they belonged to and could not be taken as representative. In practice, the group's record of cooperation with public health authorities over many years has borne out the latter assertion.[20]

As for one's religious rights, they were to be won primarily through prayer and the healing operation of God's law. Important as one's individual and institutional relations with society are, however, Christian Science shares with most traditional Christians the conviction that one's individual relationship with God is of first importance—that through the Love that *is* God we learn how really to love our fellow beings. Christian Science treatment for the sick, the sinning, the fearful, the sorrowing, the desperate, the defeated, the demented—or the merely foolish—must always start by turning to the great heart of infinite Love, the divine Father-Mother who (according to Christian Science) sees each one of us as we are in our true being.

To the really dedicated Christian Scientist, healing is a result, not a goal. It is the human change that comes from learning who and what we spiritually are, and what our neighbor and our enemy are. In Eddy's words, healing sickness is "only the bugle-call to thought and action, in the higher range of infinite goodness."[21] But she also knew that the bugle call must ring out loud and clear if thought bemused by material appearances was to be roused to challenge the whole deceptive "lie" of mortal existence. As she put it in *Science and Health:*

> To-day the healing power of Truth is widely demonstrated as an imma-
> nent, eternal Science, instead of a phenomenal exhibition. Its appearing is
> the coming anew of the gospel of "on earth peace, good-will toward men."
> This coming, as was promised by the Master, is for its establishment as a
> permanent dispensation among men; but the mission of Christian Science
> now, as in the time of its earlier demonstration, is not primarily one of
> physical healing. Now, as then, signs and wonders are wrought in the

metaphysical healing of physical disease; but these signs are only to demonstrate its divine origin,—to attest the reality of the higher mission of the Christ-power to take away the sins of the world.[22]

Without its healing record, Christian Science could be written off as a possibly beautiful but practically dangerous theory for people unable to face the facts of life. But the record was there.[23] As a result, in the half century from 1910 to 1960 the church gained wide acceptance. The international prestige of the *Monitor* helped greatly. The growth of the ecumenical movement and of the early interest of the mainline churches in spiritual healing opened a few new doors to the wider Christian community. The number of Christian Science organizations in colleges and universities around the world grew considerably, and the first faint signs of a new level of Christian Science historical scholarship began to appear. But most important was the evidence of continued good healing in the movement. The increasing recognition of this by legislatures, courts, insurance companies, and public health agencies has sometimes been attributed to skillful public relations by the church. But mere skill could never have achieved such a result in the face of the strong, articulate, organized opposition arrayed against it, unless it had been backed up by the known lives of its adherents.

At the same time, respectability brought certain dangers with it, a degree of complacency, for instance. The Church of Christ, Scientist, became associated in many people's minds with middle-class prosperity—a superficial judgment, but with a modicum of truth in it. As the historic Mrs. Eddy receded farther into history, her position as Discoverer, Founder, and Leader of the movement remained firm through the continued guidance of her writings, but there was a useful warning for the future in the otherwise wildly misleading statement of Stefan Zweig in 1931: "What was molten lava when erupted from the volcanic soul of Mary Baker Eddy, is now cold, and a tranquil fellowship of undistinguished folk has established itself on the lower slopes of the extinct crater."[24]

It was the healing work of Christian Science—healing that I have observed with wonder for almost seventy years—which more than anything else has given the lie to Zweig's statement. For such healing is work and commitment, as well as adventure. To quote Michael Drury, a spiritual healer with no definite church attachment:

> Of course we want healing, but will we put up with the work of getting there? Do we want *spiritual* healing, which means also insight and commitment and growing pains? If one is granted only miracles of sudden recovery that are completely un-understood, you are left exactly where you

were before you got sick, and the main point is lacking. God's succor is not just an isolated bounty. It is meant to grow us up, to deepen our knowledge of who we are and who God is, to increase our joy, to widen our vision.[25]

But spiritual healing is not carried on in a vacuum. During this same period of 1910–60, spirituality was under assault. Science and technology were increasingly reshaping our lives and our values. Medicine was moving toward what has been called its Golden Age, when the media would take the word *miracle* from religion and apply it to the latest achievement in medicine or surgery. The churches were already beginning to turn to advertising, promotion, and public relations as additional sacraments for the new era, while membership numbers declined.

In 1966 the Church of Christ, Scientist, celebrated the hundredth anniversary of Eddy's discovery of Christian Science. (It was announced at that time that a magnificent new church center would be built in Boston around The Mother Church and its Publishing Society, as befitting the world headquarters of a movement which had spread around the globe.) In stark contrast, the following year (1967) a Christian Science mother on Cape Cod, not far from Boston, was convicted of involuntary manslaughter for the death of her five-year-old daughter under Christian Science treatment.[26]

It was the first such verdict in Massachusetts history, though based on a 1909 statute requiring parents to provide their children with "proper physical care." The statute had never before been interpreted to mean that relying on Christian Science treatment for a child could be considered a violation of this requirement, much less a criminal offense. Indeed, the Commonwealth's policy over many years suggested just the opposite: that Christian Scientists' practice of spiritual healing in the raising of their families had met the requirement for provision of proper physical care. The Massachusetts Society for the Prevention of Cruelty to Children, which originally proposed and administered the statute, later took the same liberal position on the basis of their own reassuring experience with children under Christian Science care. There was and is no evidence of a disproportionate number of deaths resulting from this policy.

The new interpretation given to the statute by the judge in the Cape Cod case marked the first warning note of approaching changes in the mental climate. It was not met with universal approval even in the medical and public health sector. Some civil libertarians pointed to the undue burden it placed on Christian Scientists. No physician is expected to insure success in every case. To expect Christian Science practitioners to insure 100-percent success was to hold them to a standard the rest of society doesn't ask of itself.

This was sufficiently evident at the time to lead the judge to give only a suspended sentence to the mother in the case, and the Massachusetts legislature later amended the child welfare statute in question to recognize explicitly the conscientious practice of spiritual healing.

A report of the Massachusetts Department of Public Health in the *New England Journal of Medicine* of February 14, 1974, furnishes a useful example of the same spirit persisting in the face of the new aggressiveness:

> Although Massachusetts has not always led in accommodating the beliefs of minorities, it has respected philosophic and jurisdictional limits through regulation by state and local health departments. In part, this mutual tolerance owes much to the original teaching of Mrs. Eddy. . . .
>
> Christian Science in Massachusetts is careful to delineate the practice of healing from the practice of diagnostic and therapeutic medicine, a distinction recognized in the state's Medical Practice Act. Many conventional medical practitioners do not realize that such healing is covered under Blue Cross–Blue Shield and private-insurance-company group-health insurance, Workmen's Compensation and Social Security. . . . The Commonwealth recognizes the right of citizens to rely on God and to provide Christian Science care and treatment, even for minors, as long as the Department of Public Health is satisfied that the child is not neglected or lacking in proper physical care.[27]

But the climate of thought in the United States has changed radically since the Cape Cod trial. Despite the large number of young children who die under medical care every year for a variety of reasons—including iatrogenic, nosocomial, and periontogenic causes—medical prestige is so great at present that many courts, legislatures, and government agencies seem inclined to accept the view that any treatment of serious illness other than that of orthodox medicine is in fact no treatment at all.

To Christian Scientists this may seem like regression to the end of the last century, but actually the situation today is far more complex. In the 1890s the AMA in its understandable zeal to put down all forms of medical quackery had launched all-out war against Christian Science, ignoring what William James, with his own medical training and experience behind him, called the "patent and startling" cures the new religious healers were producing. It was the *facts* that counted, James insisted pragmatically, not the theory. And as the doctors pressed for laws to outlaw Christian Science healing, he burst out to a friend: "Why this mania for more laws? Why seek to stop the really extremely important experiences which these peculiar people are rolling up?"[28]

These "peculiar people" had learned a lot about their responsibilities as well as their rights in that early period. To quote Thomas Johnsen:

> The most difficult issues of responsibility then, as now, involved the care of children. Christian Scientists could understand the "honest opinion" of doctors on the necessity for medical treatment—most having earlier shared this opinion themselves. They did not believe, a church official told the *New York Evening Telegram* in 1903, that a parent simply has the right to "sacrifice" a child "to his own belief. . . . I would state without reservation that he has no such right." But neither did they feel that conscientious reliance on spiritual instead of medical means for healing should automatically be defined by the law as neglect. Their position, which sought a balance between parental and state responsibilities, received considerable support in the press, and eventually in the law. The newspaper publisher William Randolph Hearst, a non-adherent, wrote about one "miracle" in which his own infant son, in critical condition because of a closed pylorus but considered too frail to survive an operation, was healed overnight after a Christian Science practitioner was called in as a last resort. Similar experiences led other parents to feel the same kind of gratitude. . . . They held that decisions on treatment of their own children should be left to the children's "natural guardians, who are at the bedside and to whom the little one's life means more than it does to all other persons."[29]

But what of the failures, the tragic loss of a loved child? Is this not a sacrifice of the child for an abstract ideology? How can Christian Scientists live with a fact like this?

An unspoken assumption lies behind such questions: that medicine is a vastly superior and virtually infallible form of healing which could almost certainly have saved the child's life. In the 1890s it was clear to any rational observer that this was not the case. Today the magic of new cures and mechanisms tends to obscure the failures and fallibilities that attend any human activity, no matter how skilled and dedicated it may be.

The failures of medicine seldom receive the huge publicity accorded its triumphs. By contrast, the great stream of Christian Science healing through the century has received little or no attention in the mass media, and the rare occasions when a child dies under Christian Science treatment will almost invariably receive sharply adverse publicity in the press.

An ironic reverse effect is to be found in the experience of Christian Scientists, illustrating the great gap in understanding to be crossed from both sides. Through the past century thousands of people have become Christian Scientists through experiencing or witnessing a remarkable healing when Christian Science was turned to in desperation after a wholly negative medical prognosis had been received. Such people are apt to think, when they hear of a child's death in a hospital, "Oh, if only the family had been willing to try Christian Science!" But fortunately they are not likely to feel that the parents should be tried for criminal neglect because they had *not* tried it. Such an analogy may sound preposterous to many readers, and it would be if there were an inordinate death rate for Christian Science children, but there is not.

An editorial in the *Cincinnati Enquirer* in 1987 made an interesting comment on this point. The editorial had to do with a proposed bill in the Ohio General Assembly that would in effect make medical care mandatory for all children and allow no exemption for Christian Science families. The paper pointed out the difficult problem of resolving long-established legal rights that seem to be in conflict. In this case, the *Enquirer* stated, the conflict was between (1) the Constitutional guarantee of the free exercise of religion and (2) the right and responsibility of the state to intervene to protect the life and health of children. (One might add that this kind of problem involves an equally important but more pragmatic question: Is the state in a position to make an a priori decision about the relative healing merits of orthodox medicine and Christian Science?) In the course of its brief but reasonable discussion, the editorial made one especially arresting statement:

> Among those fighting the Jones bill or at least seeking an amendment, are the Christian Scientists, who have a long record of advocating spiritual healing. They can cite impressive statistics to support their claims: 24,821 children under the age of 14 have died in Ohio during the past decade, but only two of them had Christian Science parents relying on their faith's healing.[30]

Statistics can always be argued with, but the rarity of such cases as have come up in U.S. courts in the past ten years is unquestionable. Yet if trials are indeed "proofs of God's care," as *Science and Health* maintains, then there are some hard lessons for Christian Scientists to learn in demonstrating more fully both their understanding of God and their communication with society.

Although I can do no more here than touch upon so important and complex a subject, it raises questions that need much greater consideration by Christian Scientists themselves, by other spiritual healers, physicians, lawyers, legislators, bureaucrats, and the general public. So far as the subject of this book is concerned, the legal situation at this period marks a crossroads for the Christian Science tradition.

Not all those in the tradition recognize that fact yet. The writer of a 1987 editorial in the *Christian Science Sentinel* entitled "There is a battle at the crossroads" found it necessary to remind his Christian Scientist readers that for nearly a decade "court cases, public censure, and more recently even the threat of imprisonment, have been a daily way of life for a few Christian Scientists." But much more, the editorial continues, was going on than "just a small denomination's standing up to legal and bureaucratic pressures to conform." The whole of society was now being forced to confront "the greatest of questions about the nature of man." The issues at stake were no longer "the sole province of philosophers and theologians" but were intruding "practical differences in scores of everyday decisions."[31]

Although the larger issues have to do with the very survival of spiritual values in a scientific, technological, and extremely muddled world, the immediate, practical issue was addressed in a down-to-earth protest by a Christian Science grandmother in the "Rostrum" column of *U.S. News & World Report* in 1986. Lois O'Brien, for many years a teacher of rhetoric at the University of California in Davis, spoke out of long personal and family experience in Christian Science. At the same time her protest serves to illustrate the undoubted feelings of all those Christian Scientists who are alert enough to realize the new challenge facing them today in the practice of their religion. O'Brien writes:

> I'm a concerned grandmother—concerned about the way the media cover criminal prosecutions in my state, California.
>
> Several parents, who are Christian Scientists, have been charged with murder and manslaughter for turning to spiritual healing instead of seeking medical aid for a child who died.
>
> I can't speak for the parents, but as a Christian Scientist I know how much they loved these children. And I know they are not criminals any more than the many equally loving parents who have had a child die under medical care.
>
> My own family has relied on Christian Science healing for four generations. I have never considered prayer a gamble. Please understand: I'm not speaking of some crude kind of "faith healing" that implores God to heal and says it was His will if nothing happens. I'm speaking of responsible spiritual healing practiced now over a century by many perfectly normal citizens and caring parents.
>
> I'm concerned about not being taken seriously—that nobody in the media (and this includes *U.S. News & World Report*) is really taking into account that these healings have been happening over many years. Not just in my family, not just my friends. I'm speaking of the massive, long-term experience in a whole denomination.
>
> These healings just don't seem to register. Again and again, articles are written as if they had never occurred. It seems as if a portion of our society just can't stand to have its "enlightened" secular assumptions questioned by seriously considering the evidence of Christian healing in our time.

Christians in many denominations are taking spiritual healing more and more seriously. Why then should it be dismissed in the media and in the framing of public policy?

In a country founded on a quest for religious freedom, there needs to be room for differences—even major ones. This is *not* to say that religious freedom gives anyone the right to neglect or mistreat their children. Or that Christian Scientists any more than others should be given a blank ticket. But where there is a caring home environment and a track record of healing in many thousands of families, the law should not take away the choices of those who love these precious children most. Nor should the media ignore the overwhelming record of good care they have been given.[32]

This complaint is transmuted in the *Christian Science Sentinel* editorial already quoted into a more Olympian view of the situation. The writer, Allison W. Phinney, Jr.—himself a fourth-generation Christian Scientist—describes the present attack on Christian Science healing as the by-product of an overconfident technological culture. This has occurred, he points out, at the very time there is strong evidence of a reawakening vision of what humanity can be when the spiritual dimension of existence is recognized.

Do we think of human beings as complex material mechanisms whose well-being can be "taken care of" by more and more biomedical technology, the editorial asks. Then we make our laws accordingly—regarding genetic experimentation, surrogate motherhood, euthanasia, and so on. Or are our human yearnings for justice and freedom and our spiritual intuitions, prayers, and perceptions something more than the "impractical poetry" of life? Then we write our laws in another way, and society goes in a different direction:

> A basic struggle between materialism and spiritual values is going on in human consciousness. Commenting on Christ Jesus' crucifixion and resurrection, Mrs. Eddy writes, "The determination to hold Spirit in the grasp of matter is the persecutor of Truth and Love." This kind of determination is not confined to the first century of Christian experience. It is, for those with eyes to see, thematic through human history. And right now this battle wages hotly at mankind's crossroads. Those who care, those who cannot possibly want to be neutral, need to be willing to hear of it.[33]

This last admonition is obviously directed to the Christian Scientist readers of the *Sentinel* rather than to the general public, who can hardly be expected to feel the issue with the same urgency. But some recognition of the standpoint from which it speaks is necessary in order to understand the events and developments presented in the next chapter.

·10·

Decision at the Crossroads

Here I stand. I can do no otherwise; so help me, God!
—Martin Luther

Christian Science has often been lumped together with the American success philosophies and psychologies that sprang up in the late nineteenth and early twentieth century, as noted in Chapter 3. But Eddy warned that "success in error is defeat in Truth"[1] and made it clear that the aim must always be to demonstrate successfully what is true in the kingdom-of-heaven consciousness bestowed by God rather than what is merely pleasant in the mortal scene shaped by the physical senses and earthbound thinking.

For the Christian Scientist, this doesn't mean taking either an ascetic or an otherworldly view of human life. The Psalmist assures us that at God's right hand "there are pleasures forevermore." But mortals must grow in grace even to *want* those indestructible pleasures. As *Science and Health* puts it, "the good man's heaven would be a hell to the sinner." And again: "In some way, sooner or later, all must rise superior to materiality, and suffering is oft the divine agent in this elevation."[2]

At this point it may be useful to make a brief aside in order to clear up a common misconception about Christian Science. Spiritually radical as its teaching is, it is not Gnostic. It does not scornfully dismiss the whole of human experience and the natural world as mere illusion, but looks for the spiritual reality shining through the illusion and transforming human experience. When Eddy was asked, "Is it correct to say of material objects, that they are nothing and exist only in imagination?" she replied in the *Christian Science Journal*:

> *Nothing* and *something* are words which need correct definition. . . .
> Earth is more spiritually beautiful to my gaze now than when it was more

117

earthly to the eyes of Eve. . . . To take all earth's beauty into one gulp of vacuity and label beauty nothing, is ignorantly to caricature God's creation, which is unjust to human sense and to the divine realism. In our immature sense of spiritual things, let us say of the beauties of the sensuous universe: "I love your promise; and shall know, some time, the spiritual reality and substance of form, light, and color, of what I now through you discern dimly; and knowing this, I shall be satisfied."[3]

The symbolic use of the name Eve in this passage calls to mind a quatrain dashed off by a young Christian Scientist after a discussion of the passage. Described by him as an "ecological" verse and labeled "Grandmother Earth," the lines ironically suggest the reverse side of the picture:

> Every sea becomes in time a desert
> And every mountain flattens to a plain;
> Thus Nature's prodigality proves finite
> And ancient Eve pays up for raising Cain.

There is room for wit and irony in Christian Science as well as rapture. There is even—to return to the central theme of this chapter—room for suffering as an element in the self-destruction of a material sense of being. Understood that way, suffering could be called a "divine agent"—meaning not that God, the Principle of infinite good, knows or sends suffering, but that "Truth, Life, and Love" (further synonymns for God) "are a law of annihilation to everything unlike themselves."[4] This is the paradox of the cross and the crown, crucifixion and resurrection, at the heart of Christianity. It is also what lay behind the many statements by the founder of Christian Science represented by four simple lines from her poem "Mother's Evening Prayer:"

> O make me glad for every scalding tear,
> For hope deferred, ingratitude, disdain!
> Wait, and love more for every hate, and fear
> No ill,—since God is good, and loss is gain.[5]

GAINING BY LOSING

During the past few decades, church membership and attendance figures have declined in various traditional denominations. At the same time there have been unmistakable signs of a growing hunger for spirituality in large segments of society.

In a 1986 article in the *Christian Century*, Stephen Gottschalk calculated that membership in the Church of Christ, Scientist, "has been declining at about the same rate as, or slightly faster than, that of several mainline denominations."[6] Although the church *Manual* prohibits the publication of membership figures, the decline has been visible for some years in depleted attendance at services and the actual dissolving or merging of a number of branch churches and societies. These losses are offset only to a slight extent by the new branches coming into existence during the same period.

A similar decrease of practitioners listed in the *Christian Science Journal* from 4,900 to 3,200 in the past ten years is only partly offset by an increasing number of part-time practitioners. The latter are not eligible for listing in the *Journal* because their other work, by which they may earn their living, does not permit them to be available to patients at all times and to put the healing work before everything else. Only when an individual can meet the full requirements for *Journal* listing can he or she be considered a public practitioner of Christian Science.

Eddy was never greatly impressed by numbers. She borrowed from John Ruskin a sentiment which, slightly recast, became: "A small group of wise thinkers is better than a wilderness of dullards."[7] At one point she wrote that "the growth of the cause of Christian Science seems too rapid to be healthful" and added that to remedy this there should be "no proselytizing of other denominations for Christian Science teaching."[8] It was at this time of spectacular growth that she drew up the *Manual* bylaw prohibiting the reporting of membership numbers. The church was to be judged by the quality, not the quantity, of its members. She saw the pride of power, popularity, and worldly success as an even greater danger than persecution and misrepresentation, which at least kept the members spiritually alert.

In 1895 when the press paid astonished attention to the opening of the new Mother Church edifice in Boston, Eddy wrote a letter to the students who had studied under her in the Massachusetts Metaphysical College in the 1880s. First she joined with them in thanksgiving for the "continued progress and unprecedented prosperity" of the cause. But she quickly went on to remind them of "how fleeting is that which men call great; and how permanent that which God calls good." Then followed a warning, as she pointed out to them the relevance of the experience of the fishermen-disciples who toiled all night and caught no fish:

> At times, your net has been so full that it broke: human pride, creeping into its meshes, extended it beyond safe expansion; then, losing hold of divine Love, you lost your fishes, and possibly blamed others more than yourself. But those whom God makes "fishers of men" will not pull for the

shore; like Peter, they launch into the depths, cast their nets on the right side, compensate loss, and gain a higher sense of the true idea. Nothing is lost that God gives: had He filled the net, it would not have broken.[9]

In the 1920s when I was a schoolboy at the Boston Latin School and also a weekly pupil at the Mother Church Sunday School, one could feel the spiritual imperative of Eddy's teachings in the Christian Scientists one knew. Some of them had known her personally, and one felt in them the discipline and commitment of much-tried disciples. One encountered miracles of healing on all sides—except that Christian Scientists didn't see them as miracles but as the natural expressions of divine law. But one also sensed that Christian Science teaching would be unbelievable to most people without the "signs following"—the proof of what Eddy called "the superiority of spiritual power over material resistance."[10] Spirituality and healing, Christianity and science, became complementary terms.

At the same time one couldn't help wondering whether the material prosperity of the movement might not end by dulling its spirituality—a spirituality an idealistic young person might hunger for yet feel far from attaining. One read, with something like Kierkegaard's "fear and trembling," the words of *Science and Health*: "Without a fitness for holiness, we cannot receive holiness" and the sentence that followed it: "A great sacrifice of material things must precede this advanced spiritual understanding."[11] Clearly, mere yearning and blind faith could never reach that goal. Much must be lost before more could be gained.

During the 1930s the church gained modestly in numbers, but the annual rate of growth declined markedly. There was also what one might call, metaphorically if not literally, an increased suburbanization of the movement. A gap widened between Christian Science and the intellectual currents of the period. A few Christian Science lecturers might quote from Eddington, Jeans, and Einstein in an effort to bridge the gap, but physicists within the movement—and there were quite a few by that time—complained that the lecturers were reading too much into the isolated passages they quoted and that they must stop saying baldly that "even the physicists today recognize the nothingness of matter."

Although the movement was prospering moderately and its spirit remained buoyant, there were those who felt that some of the original fire had gone out of it. But when World War II came, it was clear that the fire was still there. The suffering, sacrifice, and massive hardship of that period brought forth the best of Christian Science. In Germany and Japan and the occupied countries of Europe and Asia the movement had to go underground, but there and in concentration camps, prison camps, refugee camps, in heavily bombed civilian areas and grievously overburdened field hospitals, in front-line battles and home-front struggles, Christian Scientists demonstrated remarkably the presence and power of God to heal and save and bless. Many of the recorded experiences of that time might almost belong to the Book of Acts. [12]

Here was something to challenge the sociologist's judgment that Christian Science was basically for neurotic women suffering from the tensions of modern urban living, [13] or well-to-do retirees who had never had to face serious deprivation and misery. Here, too, was evidence that once the special challenges of war were over, Christian Scientists would have to carry the same sense of urgency and total commitment into the less obviously demanding years to follow, if they were to be ready to face the ultimate decision at the crossroads.

MATERIALISM: NEW STYLE

Religion in the decades that followed the Second World War had to face two major facts of human life. One was the diabolism symbolized by Ausch-witz, Hiroshima, and the assorted moral horrors since then, including the possibility of humankind's self-annihilation, touched off by nuclear accident or madness. The other was the revolution in values resulting from the stupendous advances in science and technology. Paradoxically, those advances hold within themselves the possibility not only of liberating humanity from many of the long-accepted limitations of matter but also of locking the human race more firmly into matter by recreating mortals in the image and likeness of the mechanisms that human ingenuity has so cleverly produced. There is a childlike wisdom in the King James version of Ecclesiastes 7:29: "God hath made man upright; but they have sought out many inventions."

How did Christian Scientists look at the dizzying material changes in the years that followed VJ Day?

They looked at them, for the most part, optimistically. But optimism is not, strictly speaking, a Christian Science term. It occurs only once in all Eddy's writings, and then in a negative way. In general, optimism may be preferable to pessimism as a human attitude—as positive thinking may be preferable to negative thinking—but neither is "scientific" in the Christian Science sense of the word. From that metaphysical position, what was called for was the spiritual discrimination that could distinguish clearly between the positive and negative aspects of the technological revolution—and of the accompanying revolutions in such diverse fields as sexual mores, medicine, and theology.

There were, of course, many Christian Scientists who did make that distinction, and who saw the importance of not letting the dazzling accomplishments of human cleverness dim their recognition of the infinite power of divine Love, received directly into one's heart and life. The strong record of spiritual healing through that forty-year period showed no diminution of the Christ-power. What did show up in some parts of the movement was a weakening of commitment to the pure spirituality requisite for such healing. There was more compromise with material ways and means, more demand for aggressive promotional and public relations activities.

During the 1950s and 1960s two long series of radio and television programs, "How Christian Science Heals" and "The Bible Speaks to You," were produced by the church and bore vivid witness to both the healings and the Christianity of Christian Science. Both series brought in thousands of appreciative letters from Christian Scientists and the general public, but neither filled the churches, as had been hoped. At the time, of course, enormous media coverage was being given to the spectacular medical and surgical advances then beginning to fascinate the public. Yet this was not the sort of forum Eddy sought. She was strongly convinced that the radical spirituality of Christian Science must win its way in the face of the world's opposition on "the battleground of daily living," not "the parade ground of publicity."[14]

Some Christian Scientists during the past few decades have felt that the movement put too much emphasis on healing. Young people, they say, are mostly healthy and are simply not interested in healing. Others say that the healing emphasis is too self-centered, too concerned with the body, too materialistic. Others point to the triumphs of modern medicine and say that there is no reason today to look elsewhere for healing. Others quote Eddy's statement that physical healing is "the smallest part of Christian Science" and omit the next sentence in which she calls it "the bugle-call to thought and action, in the higher range of infinite goodness."[15]

These are definitely minority views, but they show that it is possible to think of oneself as an ardent Christian Scientist and still not grasp the radical spirituality it demands. The same thing is true of another minority in the movement who see the healing work not as a bugle call to higher spirituality but as material for a huge advertising campaign, to be accompanied with drums and trumpets and banners announcing all the diseases of which Christian Science (not God) can heal you. (I exaggerate in describing those who exaggerate, but then I remember that even these go-getters may have experienced a very wonderful healing from a very terrible disease and that their genuine gratitude needs only to be lifted and purified by further spiritual growth.)

From the Christian Science point of view, to see a spiritual healing only as a physical blessing is in itself an indication of materialistic thinking; the real importance of such healing is what it reveals about God, Spirit, as infinite good and the source of all true being. As such, the Christian Scientist feels, healing is one of the most visible and tangible signs that can be offered that the man and woman of God's creating are infinitely more than organisms or mechanisms evolved from and governed by matter.

This brings us back to the healing work of a Christian Science practitioner and to the sharp decline in the number of practitioners listed in the monthly *Journal*. The decline is certainly not the result of a lack of patients: there is a crying demand in the movement for more practitioners, and a good one almost anywhere will be swamped with requests for help. But to go "into the practice," as Christian Scientists say, is a total commitment. It requires (to use Eddy's word) an "unselfed" dedication to the work, the same courage, fidelity, and readiness to respond to any kind of emergency that many Christian Scientists demonstrated in relation to the inescapable demands of wartime situations.

In the more relaxed conditions of peacetime civilian life it is easier for even an earnest Christian Scientist who yearns to go into the practice to take refuge in the argument: "I'm not ready yet. I'm not good enough. I'm not sure that I could do this and take care of my family responsibilities, too." Or even, "Do I dare take the risks I may encounter? Here in my office I can press a few buttons on my computer and get instant retrieval of information I need. But in a practitioner's office could I be as sure in my prayer of receiving the precise truths that are needed to bring healing to someone in a desperate situation?" And so on. If a person really isn't ready, these arguments may be simple common sense. At other times they may reveal that what is really demanded is a stronger sense of urgency concerning the world's pitiful need for the spiritual healing of its woes.

By the 1960s the Boston headquarters of the movement was moving in two directions. On the one hand, it had hired a leading management consultant firm to tell it how to run its business more effectively. On the other hand, it was supporting an independent research project that involved digging more deeply into Eddy's own views on how her church should be run. The results were, as might be expected, fairly antipodal. And what ensued was not a clear-cut choice between the two but an attempt to accommodate both points of view.

One of the arguments advanced for bringing in the management consultants was that the matter had been prayed about and that the decision to take the step had come as the direct result of that prayer. Unfortunately the ultimate results cast doubt on the adequacy of the prayer. After some years of drastic change engineered by the consultants, the church situation had deteriorated rather than improved. Many of the proposed plans simply didn't work, and almost all of them were eventually discarded. Many of the employees in the Boston headquarters complained that they no longer felt they were working for a church, but for a business—and an ailing business at that. The concept of strategic five-year plans which Western society had borrowed from Josef Stalin proved incompatible with Eddy's basic concept of spiritual demonstration, and eventually almost everyone agreed that the 1960s experiment had been a failure.

Eddy's view is summed up very forcefully in an untitled manuscript that came to light in the church archives during the research on this subject. She apparently wrote this unpublished paper in the early 1890s when she was constantly having to restrain her early publisher, William G. Nixon, from trying to promote the sale of *Science and Health* by commercial schemes of which she disapproved. God's ways, she had written Nixon, were entirely "opposed to your worldly material means," and she could not permit him to "have in business the same material motives that the world acts from." This point is developed further in the unpublished manuscript:

> The smartest business man is not scientifically a safe business man. He is not as smart as God, while he thinks himself smarter and is quite unconscious of this thought.
>
> If you have more faith in establishing Christ's Church by material organization than upon the spiritual Rock of Christ, then you build upon matter instead of Spirit and build upon sand. Personal combinations, human thought and effort, material ways and means whereby to establish and maintain the Church of Christ are weak, vacillating, temporal, subject to divisions, factions, feuds, and all the *etcetera* of mortal and material phenomena.
>
> The church created, founded and erected on the Rock against which the winds and waves prevail not, is the Church triumphant, the indwelling temple of God; it is the mind that has consecrated its affections, its aims, ambitions, hopes, joys and fruition in Spirit, whose methods and means, plans and successes are secure; they cannot be separated from success. . . .
>
> What is your model business man—the real Scientist who plants in Mind, God, who sows in Mind and reaps in Mind, or he who begins with political economy, human plans, legal speculations, and ends with them, dust to dust?[16]

Another letter written to Nixon in the same period offers a practical illustration of her own intelligence in business matters. As publisher of the *Christian Science Journal*, he had sent off a new editor to travel around the country rustling up subscriptions. Eddy finally wrote him objecting to this and giving the following warning: "If she [the editor] gets 10,000 subscribers for the [*Journal*] it will not change my views. They will be lost again unless the [*Journal*] deserves them. You look at effects, I at *cause*."[17] This wisdom was not always shared by those of her followers who thought primarily in terms of packaging, promoting, and marketing Christian Science to the world.

Through most of the century many kind things have been said about Christian Scientists as people—as citizens, neighbors, friends, colleagues. When Christian Scientists have been harshly criticized, the attack has usually been on them collectively—as an organized body, a potential power group, an irrational "cult," a slick business enterprise. Mark Twain set the pattern early in the century. After hurling invective at Eddy and her church officers, he could pay the most gracious sort of tribute to the Christian Scientists he had actually known. Another classic example, typical of many critics before and since, occurs in *Psychology, Religion and Healing*, a book by a highly respected British Methodist leader, Leslie Weatherhead, who after presenting a scathing picture of Christian Science and Eddy—factually inaccurate to an extraordinary degree—went on to say:

> While we may criticise many things in Christian Science, I must pay tribute here to the characters of Christian Scientists. Those I have met have not seemed proud or intolerant. They have seemed to me humble, inwardly serene and radiant, and to be in touch with spiritual resources which are all too commonly untapped. Their conception of the reality and power of God is finer than most, and rids their minds of fear. In the main they seem healthy, loving and forgiving people, practised in the discipline of excluding from themselves "hatred, malice and all uncharitableness." Above all they appear to me really to love others in the Christian sense and I am more and more convinced of the therapeutic energies released by such loving.[18]

These are virtues that nurture Christian healing individually, but they are not sufficient of themselves to carry forward and protect an organized movement dedicated to a view of reality which directly challenges basic assumptions of the scientific-technological orthodoxy that dominates society today. The logic of Christian Science demands that an ailing church be treated as an ailing patient would be—with total commitment to spiritual ways and means, not human skills and repairs. Healing through prayer is still at the heart of living Christian Science, collectively no less than individually.

To some Christian Scientists it seemed that if the church looked too much to outside experts for solutions to its organizational, financial, and public relations and membership problems, this would be roughly equivalent to a member's running off to try the latest fashionable medical treatment if he or she wasn't receiving the looked-for quick healing through Christian Science treatment. In either case, according to basic Christian Science teaching, the real need might be for greater spiritual regeneration, for more "unselfed love," moral courage, or Christian humility. The individual member was free to make his or her decision about which way to go; the church, under the *Manual,* was committed to the more spiritual way.

In a 1977 pamphlet entitled *Mary Baker Eddy: Discoverer, Founder, Leader,* the statement is made that one of the founder's basic aims in the *Manual* was to keep the church "responsive to divine direction, mindful at all times of its Christian, healing purpose, intent on the spiritualization of human thought rather than on the accumulation of power, wealth, numbers, prestige." Then follow two paragraphs that sum up much of what I have tried to convey in the above few pages:

> In providing for its outreach to the world, she took unending care to guard against the kind of attrition through acculturation which once before had all but drained Christianity of its radical healing vitality. She clearly expected Christian Science to come to the rescue of the Christian churches, beleaguered by the world's increasing secularism. She fully intended the Church of Christ, Scientist, to show a better way, not join in the frantic scurry for humanistic solutions to problems built into the presuppositions of materiality.
>
> As Founder, Mrs. Eddy had a keen historical sense of how the early Christian Church, in its effort to win the great pagan world about it, had embraced the very tendencies it had set out to heal. With prophetic insight, she also foresaw the fruitless scramble for mortal mind's attention and approval that would mark the besieged Christianity of the twentieth century—the tired old pattern of compromise disguised as a smart new adventure in self-defeat. The straight and narrow way of the *Manual,* she made clear, was the radical way of unlimited demonstration.[19]

MONITOR AND MANUAL

One month after the first issue of the *Christian Science Monitor* came off the press on November 25, 1908, a Christian Scientist wrote in the weekly *Christian Science Sentinel:*

Our Leader's request that "every Christian Scientist . . . subscribe for and read our daily newspaper" (*Sentinel*, Nov. 21) is a call to a higher privilege, and the significance of this request is gradually assuming more and more definite proportions. . . . The first conspicuous effect of this wonderful gift to ourselves and to the world has been to lift one's eyes to an horizon far beyond one's own doorstep. The call to help in the world's thinking is no longer something that can pass unheeded, it is an imperative duty. Things we did not like to look at nor think of, problems we did not feel able to cope with, must now be faced manfully, and correct thinking concerning the world's doings cultivated and maintained.[20]

The word *manfully* may be significant. The great majority of Christian Science practitioners were women. The feminist Mary Burt Messer wrote later that Christian Science "confirms the age-old association of woman with the ministry of love."[21] But eighty years ago this ministry was still most clearly manifest in relation to the individual, the family, the neighborhood, the local church; world outreach and business leadership were still masculine prerogatives.

William Nixon, Eddy's early publisher who had resisted her spiritual guidance in such matters, had finally turned against her bitterly and left Christian Science; his wife, Helen, who remained a faithful Christian Science practitioner and teacher all her life, was the writer of the above passage, and her use of the word *manfully* suggests that she understood a frequently overlooked statement in *Science and Health:* "Let the 'male and female' of God's creating appear."[22] Possibly something of the same kind was in the mind of Clara Barton, founder and first president of the American Red Cross, when she said of the founder of Christian Science: "Love permeates all the teachings of this great woman,—so great, I believe, that at this perspective we can scarcely realize how great."[23] A few months later the "great woman" launched the *Christian Science Monitor:* "to injure no man but to bless all mankind."[24]

Before many years went by, the paper was winning international acclaim, and later it began to appear on lists of the ten best newspapers in the world. From the outset Eddy had definite ideas about what the paper should be. It should have intellectual excellence as well as broad family appeal. It should not flinch from bad news and tough issues, but neither should it exploit or sensationalize them. In facing the problems of the world, it should be neither a Cassandra nor a Pollyanna. It should not preach Christian Science, but it should look for constructive possibilities in even the most difficult situations.

In 1910, a few months before Eddy's death in her ninetieth year, Alfred Farlow of the Committee on Publication wrote her: "It is wonderful what the

Monitor is doing as a missionary. . . . It is a better missionary than the Christian Scientists because it does not talk too much; it does not commit Christian Science unwisely, and does not disgrace us by unwise answers to insincere questions of critics."[25]

After Eddy's passing, the brilliant British journalist Frederick Dixon, whom she had called to Boston when she started the *Monitor* and who became its editor in 1914, wrote with typical coolness in the London *Outlook* concerning her leadership and the "body of devoted assistants" around her: "No matter how hard they might work, she worked harder still; and for months and years, while they were receiving her constant and incisive instructions, they read with mingled amusement and amazement the stories of her mental incapacity and the failure of the movement, which then, very much as now, constituted in the press the news of Christian Science."[26]

The founder of Christian Science had faced up "manfully" to the problems of her movement and of the world, but her leadership rested squarely on her spiritual intuition and perception rather than on a mastery of worldly ways and means. It was generally understood that this spiritual leadership would continue to operate through the rules and bylaws of the *Manual of The Mother Church* which she had provided for the future guidance of the movement. A "mother" church must necessarily express the cherishing, healing, enfolding qualities of spiritual womanhood as well as embracing the bold, venturesome thrust of ideal manhood.

MALE AND FEMALE

According to Christian Science, the two sets of values are one in God as Father-Mother, and therefore in every individual expression or reflection of God's being. But to demonstrate this in a church organization or a daily newspaper has been a stiff challenge. As the years went on, the male element in the Boston organization clearly held the reins, even under the restraints of the *Manual*. There was not a woman on the Christian Science Board of Directors until 1919, on the Board of Trustees of the Christian Science Publishing Society until 1945, as editor of the religious periodicals of the Publishing Society until 1959, and as editor of the *Christian Science Monitor* until 1983.

These figures are only symptomatic of the degree to which "masculine" reasoning and values have tended to outweigh "feminine" spirituality and insight in the running of the organization through the years. However, a fair number of men serving in these positions—or as Christian Science teachers, lecturers, practitioners, and writers for the periodicals—have certainly been quite as spiritually minded as the women who have served the organization. Eddy wrote in the last year of her life, "The male element is a strong supporting arm to religion as well as to politics, and we need in our ranks of divine energy, the strong, the faithful, the untiring spiritual armament."[27] But she also made clear in many ways in many places the need of all for the humility, patience, love, and spirituality of woman "last at the cross and first at the sepulchre." Her command was to *let* "the 'male and female' of God's creating appear."

A good example of the blending of the two was in Alfred Farlow's work in the Committee on Publication to correct public misconceptions and misrepresentations of Christian Science. In 1914 Farlow wrote an article describing his many years of experience in dealing with the press. In it he explained:

> I made no effort to effect an untimely introduction of Christian Science in the newspapers or other periodicals, nor to intrude it upon the public in any way. I held the opinion that the subject should be discussed only where it was welcome. I regarded Christian Science in human consciousness as one might a plant which is destined to thrive and grow with the sole help of God's sunshine and rain, while human hands are restrained from meddling with it and from injuring its tender shoots and branches. I entertained the opinion that Christian Science would make its way in the world because of its healing efforts and would be known by its fruits, and that our neighbors would be attracted to it by reason of its good works, and the teaching and preaching were for those who called for it, but I discovered that if misstatements were allowed to remain uncorrected the tendency was to engender bitterness and crush out toleration.[28]

To some of his fellow Christian Scientists, especially business-oriented males, Farlow's gentle approach seemed not aggressive enough. However, during his sixteen years as manager of the Committee on Publication the church grew with greater rapidity than at any other period of its history. The quiet reasonableness of his "corrective" letters to the press won both him and Christian Science a great deal of respect among editors across the country, and Eddy recognized in him the kind of "strong supporting arm" she looked for in the "male element." At the same time he shared her deep womanly conviction that it was spirituality and healing rather than promotion and publicity that would really carry the movement forward. In *Science and Health* she had written, "When God called the author to proclaim His Gospel to this age, there came also the charge to plant and water His vineyard."[29] The gardener image is one that Farlow used in the passage quoted above, and it suggests that he shared with her the concept of church development as something to be lovingly tended rather than expertly blue-printed.

As the years went on and the movement grew in numbers[30] and public acceptance, its success had a somewhat heady effect. Some church members began stepping up their demand for more publicity, more high-powered promotion that would sweep the whole of Christendom into the church. The same sort of demand had been knocked down repeatedly by Eddy, who felt that the movement was already growing too rapidly for its health.[31] It was also this kind of zeal without wisdom among many church members that had caused Farlow to write Eddy that the *Monitor* was "a better missionary than the Christian Scientists."

In the years between the surge of spiritual growth in World War II and the present time, the apparent diminishing of vitality in the movement has caused a good deal of soul-searching among those who recognized the situation. The experience with the imported management consultants in the 1960s taught an expensive lesson, but there has been disagreement about what the lesson was! To some the experience was evidence that the world's ways are not God's way of carrying forward a movement based on Spirit as All-in-all. To others it suggested that the 1960s experiment was not sufficiently thorough and knowledgeable, and that what is needed today is a complete reorganization and redirection of the church, utilizing the very latest expertise in management, strategic planning, advertising, public relations, psychology, marketing, electronic communication, computer science, global telethons, together with a more relaxed standard of traditional moral and intellectual values.

This does not mean that there is a split in the Church of Christ, Scientist. There are few Christian Scientists who would deny that the printed word may well be supplemented by the audiovisual media in conveying something of the church's message to the world on a larger scale. They also see the possibilities of this in connection with the *Monitor* news—although most feel strongly that this must not be at the expense of the daily newspaper Eddy founded. Many of the rank and file accept these giant-sized experiments with awed enthusiasm, trusting that the results will justify the radical reorientation of effort and the many millions of dollars being poured into the experiment at the time of this writing.

On the other hand, few Christian Scientists would deny that Christian healing is still at the heart of their religion. This necessarily includes healing their own churches of any materialistic pressures, attractions, or soporifics that may be depleting their numbers and weakening their spirituality. Even those who most ardently welcome the concept of reaching out to the whole world by shortwave radio and television know that the message would be empty unless backed by an increase in the spiritual beauty and healing power of their own lives as committed Christian Scientists. It is obvious that one cleans up one's own backyard before going out to tell others how to clean up theirs.

The Christian Science tradition is one of "demonstration." It is now being augmented by experimentation. A critic of Christian Science might assume that the whole history of the movement is a prolonged experiment. I would say that its very survival has been a demonstration—practical evidence of the "superiority of spiritual power over material resistance." The challenges ahead are very great. There are enormous lessons for Christian Scientists to learn in their adjustment to the mental and moral changes of our bewildering times, and enormous lessons for technocrats to learn in their adjustment to causative factors which their present theories simply cannot allow for.

I find many Christian Scientists today growing wonderfully in spiritual strength and depth as they face today's challenges. I think of Jesus saying to his disciples *before* the crucifixion and therefore before the resurrection, "In the world ye shall have tribulation: but be of good cheer; I have overcome the world." And Paul: "I take pleasure in infirmities, in reproaches, in necessities, in persecutions, in distresses for Christ's sake: for when I am weak, then am I strong." And Eddy in commenting on Paul: "Christians to-day should be able to say, with the sweet sincerity of the apostle, 'I take pleasure in infirmities,'—I enjoy the touch of weakness, pain, and all suffering of the flesh, *because* it compels me to seek the remedy for it, and to find happiness, apart from the personal senses."[32]

That, in turn, brings to mind a passage I wrote thirty years ago for my first book on Christian Science. Following a chapter called "The Pragmatic Test," which dealt with the evidence for Christian Science healing, the passage, written on sudden impulse, stated that

> beyond all the careful calculations of scientific credibility and pragmatic usefulness, our sense of fitness demands that the highest spiritual values shall have a quality of *daring*, a total commitment to God regardless of what may be the practical result. Luther expressed it in his demand for a "daring, reckless confidence in the grace of God." Job said with stark simplicity: "Though he slay me, yet will I trust in him."
>
> This is the spirit of Christian Science at its point of departure from the world of the senses. It leaves all for God, all the lesser comforts, all the easy compromises. If a man's spiritual understanding prove unequal to the physical challenge that confronts him, then he may choose to suffer what appears to the world as defeat rather than doubt the omnipotence of Love

or its willingness to heal him. If his courage fail, he may yet summon up new spiritual strength from the depths of a conviction so wholly anchored in the divine that it has no taint of human pride or will or weakness. And in this very abandonment to the love of God, in this very acknowledgment of utter helplessness to be or do anything that He has not purposed, a man may find the revelation of a good beyond anything he has dared to hope. It is at the moment of total self-surrender that the fountaining joy at the heart of existence leaps forth as healing, as resurrection, as victory.[33]

Thirty years later, this seems to me a very male statement. Written out of experience and with a heart full of gratitude, it expresses something of the depth of one kind of individual experience. But it takes no account of the social matrix in which decisions must be made, the family situations, the age, experience, and spiritual readiness of the individual who must make the decision. One certainly wouldn't want anyone to take such an absolute stand out of sheer bravado.

In short, this kind of statement needs to be balanced by the intuitive mother-love that cares for the individual's various stages of advance and changing relations to the environment. At the level of the collective, this "woman" quality ideally coordinates and embraces the whole situation, as Jane Addams's social vision embraced her very practical Hull House activities in Chicago's slums. In Eddy's case, her vision of the spiritual Church Universal and Triumphant as embracing the whole human family led to the close and constant attention she gave to the practical relations of her church organization with the society, or societies, in which it operated. She knew that the church must meet the pragmatic as well as the spiritual test, hence the time and care she devoted to the *Manual of The Mother Church* in the last fifteen years of her life.

The *Manual*, she wrote, did not originate "in solemn conclave," nor was it the outcome of what today would be called strategic planning. Its bylaws, in her words, were "not arbitrary opinions nor dictatorial demands, such as one person might impose on another. They were impelled by a power not one's own, were written at different dates, and as the occasion required. They sprang from necessity, the logic of events,—from the immediate demand for them as a help that must be supplied to maintain the dignity and defense of our Cause. . . ."[34] Of the *Manual* in relation to the movement as a whole, she wrote, "It stands alone, uniquely adapted to form the budding thought and hedge it about with divine Love."[35] And again: "Of this I am sure, that each Rule and By-law in this Manual will increase the spirituality of him who obeys it, invigorate his capacity to heal the sick, to comfort such as mourn, and to awaken the sinner."[36]

Strange as it may seem, that little book—not the church officers who are its administrators or the members who subscribe to its tenets and bylaws when they join—is the final authority in the church. It may well be the *Manual* that decides which way the Christian Science movement will go at the crossroads. The original impetus of the movement took the church down the road "less traveled."[37] The question now is whether it can reach its destination more rapidly and more easily by turning onto the six-lane highway where the mainstream of twentieth-century traffic so confidently flows.

Notes

Introduction

1. Mary Baker Eddy, *Manual of The Mother Church* (Boston: The First Church of Christ, Scientist, 1936), p. 17; hereafter cited as *Manual*.
2. Mary Baker Eddy, *Science and Health with Key to the Scriptures* (Boston: The First Church of Christ, Scientist, 1934), p. 453; hereafter cited as *Science and Health*.

Chapter 1/Christian Science: Theology or Therapy?

1. Mary Baker Eddy, *Retrospection and Introspection* (Boston: The First Church of Christ, Scientist, 1920), p. 24; hereafter cited as *Retrospection*.
2. Quoted in Robert Peel, *Mary Baker Eddy: The Years of Discovery* (New York: Holt, Rinehart and Winston, 1958), pp. 101–2; hereafter cited as *Mary Baker Eddy I*. The original article was published in *I.O.O.F. Covenant* (Baltimore), May 1847.
3. Ralph Waldo Emerson, *Nature, Addresses and Lectures* (Cambridge, Mass.: Belknap Press, 1879).
4. Eddy, *Retrospection*, p. 31.
5. H. A. L. Fisher, *Our New Religion* (New York: Jonathan Cape and Harrison Smith, 1930), pp. 41, 60.
6. For further background on the relation of Evans to Quimby see Peel, *Mary Baker Eddy I*, pp. 189–90, 301–3.
7. Quoted from Quimby manuscripts in Annetta G. Dresser, *The Philosophy of P. P. Quimby* (Boston: George H. Ellis, 1895), p. 87.
8. Fisher, *Our New Religion*, p. 25.
9. Peel, *Mary Baker Eddy I*, p. 180.
10. *The Quimby Manuscripts*, ed. Horatio W. Dresser (New York: Thomas Y. Crowell, 1921), pp. 118–19.

11. Peel, *Mary Baker Eddy I*, p. 183. Full statement in Document A&M6-10242 in Mother Church Archives.

12. Mary Baker Eddy, *Miscellaneous Writings* (Boston: The First Church of Christ, Scientist, 1924), p. 24.

13. Karl Holl, "Der Szientismus," *Gesammelte Aufsätze zur Kirchengeschichte* (Tübingen, 1921–28), 3:460–79.

14. Quoted in Peel, *Mary Baker Eddy I*, p. 203.

15. Quoted in Peel, *Mary Baker Eddy I*, p. 212.

16. Quoted in Peel, *Mary Baker Eddy I*, pp. 209–10.

Chapter 2/The Word Made Flesh

1. *Ecumenical Papers* (Boston: Christian Science Publishing Society, 1969), pp. 36–44.

2. Holl, "Der Szientismus," 3:460–79.

3. Paul Tillich, "Reinhold Niebuhr's Doctrine of Knowledge," in *Reinhold Niebuhr: His Religious, Social, and Political Thought*, ed. Charles W. Kegley and Robert W. Bretall (New York: Macmillan, 1956), p. 41.

4. Eddy, *Science and Health*, p. 116.

5. Perry Miller, *The New England Mind: The Seventeenth Century* (New York: Macmillan, 1930), p. 9.

6. *Ecumenical Papers*, p. 32.

7. Quoted in Peel, *Mary Baker Eddy I*, p. 57.

8. C. S. Lewis, *Miracles: A Preliminary Study* (New York: Macmillan, 1947), pp. 93, 94.

9. Eddy, *Miscellaneous Writings*, p. 82.

10. Werner Heisenberg, *Physics and Beyond* (New York: Harper and Row, 1971), pp. 88, 89.

11. Romans 8:1, 2 (New English Bible). All biblical quotations in this book are from the King James Version unless otherwise identified, as here.

12. Karl Holl, "Der Szientismus," 3:460–79.

13. Eddy, *Science and Health*, pp. 25, 350.

14. Ibid., p. 34.

15. Ibid., p. 561.

16. Stephen Gottschalk, "Theodicy after Auschwitz and the Reality of God," *Union Seminary Quarterly Review* 41, nos. 3 and 4 (1987): 77–91.

17. Allison W. Phinney, Jr., in *The Christian Science Monitor*, 31 January 1963.

18. Eddy, *Science and Health*, p. 313.

Chapter 3/Being and Well-Being

1. Eddy, *Science and Health*, pp. 238, 575, 15, 36; *Miscellaneous Writings*, pp. 138, 397; *Science and Health*, p. 179.

2. Eddy, *Science and Health*, p. 26.

3. William James, *The Varieties of Religious Experience* (London and New York: Longmans, Green, 1929).

4. Eddy, *Retrospection*, p. 23.

5. Review by Raymond J. Cunningham of Peel, *Mary Baker Eddy I*, in *American Historical Review*, April 1967.

6. Robert Peel, *Mary Baker Eddy: The Years of Trial* (New York: Holt, Rinehart and Winston, 1971), p. 228; hereafter cited as *Mary Baker Eddy II*.

7. Sydney E. Ahlstrom, *A Religious History of the American People* (New Haven: Yale University Press, 1972). Charles S. Braden, *Spirits in Rebellion* (Dallas: Southern Methodist University Press, 1963).

8. Eddy, *Science and Health*, p. 327.

9. Eddy, *Message to The Mother Church for 1901* (Boston: The First Church of Christ, Scientist, 1901), p. 15.

10. Stephen Gottschalk, *The Emergence of Christian Science in American Religious Life* (Berkeley and Los Angeles: University of California Press, 1973), pp. 292–93.

11. Ibid., p. 113.

12. Robert Peel, *Mary Baker Eddy: The Years of Authority* (New York: Holt, Rinehart and Winston, 1977), p. 336; hereafter cited as *Mary Baker Eddy III*.

13. George Santayana, *Character and Opinion in the United States* (New York: Scribner, 1920), pp. 188–89.

14. Eddy, *Science and Health*, pp. 667–69.

15. Eddy, *Miscellaneous Writings*, p. 15.

16. *A Century of Christian Science Healing* (Boston: Christian Science Publishing Society, 1966), pp. 250, 251.

17. Hermann Keyserling, *America Set Free* (London: Jonathan Cape, 1930), pp. 457–62.

18. William Barrett, *The Death of the Soul* (Garden City, N.Y.: Anchor Press, 1986).

Chapter 4/Sexuality and Spirituality

1. Cyrus Bartol, *The Rising Faith* (Boston: Roberts Bros., 1873), p. 121.

2. Galatians 3:28 (New English Bible).

3. Eddy, *Science and Health*, p. 475.

4. Eddy, *Miscellaneous Writings*, p. 96.

5. Eddy, *Science and Health*, pp. 57, 63, 485.

6. Allison W. Phinney, Jr., then manager of the Christian Science Committee on Publication, in the *Boston Globe*, 9 June 1982, p. 45.

7. Eddy, *Science and Health*, p. 61.

8. Eddy, *The First Church of Christ, Scientist, and Miscellany* (Boston: The First Church of Christ, Scientist, 1941), p. 5; hereafter cited as *First Church and Miscellany*.

9. Eddy, *Miscellaneous Writings*, p. 52.

10. Margery Fox, "Protest in Piety: Christian Science Revisited," *International Journal of Women's Studies*, July/August 1978. Gail Parker, "Mary Baker Eddy and

Sentimental Womanhood," *New England Quarterly*, March 1970. Janice Klein, "Ann Lee and Mary Baker Eddy: The Parenting of New Religions," *Journal of Psychohistory*, Winter 1978.

11. Rosemary Radford Ruether and Rosemary Skinner Keller, *Women and Religion in America, Volume 1: The Nineteenth Century* (San Francisco: Harper and Row, 1981), pp. 48, 52.

12. Eddy, *Science and Health*, pp. 517, 64.

13. Jean McDonald, "Mary Baker Eddy and the Nineteenth-Century 'Public' Woman," *Journal of Feminist Studies in Religion* 2 (Spring 1986): 89–111.

14. Mary Burt Messer, *The Family in the Making* (New York: G. P. Putnam's Sons, 1928) pp. 351–54. See also Messer, *The Science of Society* (New York: Philosophical Library, 1959).

15. John Updike, *Roger's Version* (New York: Knopf, 1986), p. 144.

Chapter 5/Science and Health

1. Quoted in Arthur Koestler, *The Roots of Coincidence* (London: Hutchinson, 1972), p. 90.

2. René Dubos, *Mirage of Health* (New York: Harper and Bros., 1959), p. 17.

3. Derek Bok, "Needed: A New Way to Train Doctors," President's Report to the Harvard Board of Overseers, 1982–83, *Harvard Magazine*, May–June 1984, p. 38.

4. Messer, *Family in the Making*, p. 353.

5. Mary Baker Eddy, *Pulpit and Press* (Boston: The First Church of Christ, Scientist, 1923), p. 22.

6. "Christian Science and spiritual healing today: a conversation with the Reverend Paul Higgins." *Christian Science Sentinel*, 6 October 1986, pp. 1857–64. See also two reports of dialogue with Christian healers of various other denominations in *Christian Science Sentinel*, 7 and 14 December 1987.

7. Eddy, *Science and Health*, p. 134.

8. Ibid., p. 150.

9. *A Century of Christian Science Healing* (Boston: Christian Science Publishing Society, 1966), p. 254.

10. Ibid., p. 237.

11. Ibid., pp. 254–55. This same case, with a few further details, is recounted in a book dealing with many kinds of spiritual healing: Will Oursler, *The Healing Power of Faith* (New York: Hawthorn Books, 1957), pp. 111–12.

12. Eddy, *Science and Health*, p. 468.

13. Eddy, *Retrospection*, p. 93.

14. Eddy, *Science and Health*, p. 127.

15. Ibid., p. 466.

16. Mary Baker Eddy, *Rudimental Divine Science* (Boston: The First Church of Christ, Scientist, 1936), p. 2.

17. *Christian Science Hymnal* (Boston: Christian Science Publishing Society, 1937), p. 308.

18. Karl Barth, *The Word of God and the Word of Man* (New York: Harper and Bros., 1957), p. 108.

Chapter 6/Mortality, Suffering, Madness, Malice

1. Mary Baker Glover, *Science and Health*, 1st ed. (Boston: Christian Scientist Publishing Co., 1875), p. 265.

2. Eddy, *Science and Health*, pp. 476, 171.

3. Ralph Waldo Emerson, epigraph for *Nature*, first printed privately in 1836, then published in *Nature, Addresses and Lectures*, 1849.

4. Quoted in F. O. Matthiessen, *American Renaissance* (New York: Oxford University Press, 1941), p. 491.

5. This wording—first used, I believe, by Edmund W. Sinnott in his *Matter, Mind and Man* (New York: Harper and Bros., 1957)—has served as a convenient bridge for discussions between physicists, biologists, and Christian Scientists.

6. Paul Davies, *God and the New Physics* (New York: Simon and Schuster, 1983), p. 8. Harold Morowitz, "Rediscovering the Mind," in *The Mind's I*, ed. D. R. Hofstadter and D. C. Dennett (New York: Harvester/Basic Books, 1981). Nick Herbert, *Quantum Reality* (Garden City, N.Y.: Anchor Press, Doubleday, 1985).

7. Eddy, *Science and Health*, p. 119.

8. Ibid., p. 272.

9. Ibid., pp. 172, 180.

10. For a further development of this crucial theological point see Eddy's treatment of the atonement in her book *No and Yes* (Boston: The First Church of Christ, Scientist, 1936), pp. 33–38.

11. Eddy, *Science and Health*, pp. 411, 23.

12. Ibid., p. 475.

13. Ibid., pp. 53, 48, 49.

14. Ronald Goetz, "The Suffering God: The Rise of a New Orthodoxy," *Christian Century*, 16 April 1986, p. 385.

15. Quoted in Goetz, "The Suffering God," p. 388.

16. Ibid. This thought receives its noblest expression in Dietrich Bonhoeffer's *Letters and Papers from Prison* (London: SCM Press, 1955).

17. *Ecumenical Papers*, pp. 10, 12.

18. Ibid., pp. 12, 13.

19. Eddy, *Science and Health*, pp. 366–67.

20. Ibid., p. 421.

21. Ibid., pp. 454, 414.

22. *A Century of Christian Science Healing*, pp. 245–46.

23. Eddy, *Science and Health*, p. 407.

24. Eddy, *Miscellaneous Writings*, p. 369.

25. These charges of delusion were revived and spelled out in detail in Edwin F. Dakin, *Mrs. Eddy* (New York: Scribner, 1929), pp. 434–39. First came the "fundamental delusion" of the nonexistence of the physical universe, and all the others were held to have followed from that supposed cosmic gaffe. Next came the delusion that she was selected by God to receive divine revelations, a delusion as to the cause, cure, and prevention of disease, a delusion as to the operation of a diabolism she called "malicious animal magnetism," and finally the twin paranoiac delusions of grandeur and persecution. Some of the crucial documents, court records, psychiatric reports, newspaper interviews, and other evidence that Dakin chose to ignore are to

be found in Michael Meehan, *Mrs. Eddy and the Late Suit in Equity*, privately printed in Concord in 1908 but available in many rare book collections. See also Hugh A. Studdert Kennedy, *Mrs. Eddy* (San Francisco: Farallon Press, 1947), pp. 435–65; Peel, *Mary Baker Eddy III*, pp. 275–91, 480–90 (nn. 85–120).

26. See the stenographic account of this hearing in Meehan, *Mrs. Eddy and the Late Suit in Equity*, pp. 153–66, summed up in Ernest Sutherland Bates and John V. Dittemore, *Mary Baker Eddy* (New York: Knopf, 1932), p. 413: "As everyone by now expected, the result was a complete vindication of Mrs. Eddy. The only sign of weakness displayed was the slight deafness to which she confessed, which sometimes necessitated the repetition of a question. She greeted her visitors with the air of a gracious hostess, and, despite their efforts to maintain the frigid decorum of a court-room, she soon carried the interview into the easy atmosphere of an afternoon call."

27. See Peel, *Mary Baker Eddy III*, p. 485 n. 115.

28. Quoted in Robert Peel, *Christian Science: Its Encounter with American Culture* (New York: Henry Holt, 1958), p. 68; hereafter cited as *Encounter*.

29. Eddy, *Science and Health*, p. 327.

30. *Understanding Our Century*, ed. Earl W. Foell (Boston: Christian Science Publishing Society, 1984), pp. 113–14.

31. Eddy, *Miscellaneous Writings*, p. 124.

Chapter 7/Passage to the Light

1. Eddy, *Science and Health*, pp. 246, 566.

2. Eddy, *Miscellaneous Writings*, p. 15.

3. Ibid.

4. Robert Peel, *Spiritual Healing in a Scientific Age* (San Francisco: Harper and Row, 1987), pp. 116–19.

5. James Llewellyn Heiland, testimony in *Christian Science Sentinel*, 22 September 1986, pp. 1773–74.

6. Jane W. Lacey, testimony in *Christian Science Sentinel*, 7 October 1985, pp. 1725–27.

7. Full account quoted in Peel, *Encounter*, pp. 223–25, from the Wellesley (Massachusetts) *Townsman* of 31 May 1956.

8. *Living Christian Science*, ed. Marcy Babbitt (Englewood Cliffs, N.J.: Prentice-Hall, 1975), pp. 19–31.

9. Eddy, *Science and Health*, p. 574.

10. *Poems of Gerard Manley Hopkins*, ed. Robert Bridges and W. H. Gardner (New York and London: Oxford University Press, 1948), p. 64.

11. Talk given by Cleo N. Lawrence of Rome, New York, in a radio/TV series, "How Christian Science Heals," 1960. Later printed in *A Century of Christian Science Healing*, pp. 222–25.

12. Eddy, *Science and Health*, p. 246.

13. *Christian Science Sentinel*, 23 January 1965.

14. Louise W. C. Hovnanian, *The Passing of the Sea Gull* (Boston: Christian Science Publishing Society, 1927).

Chapter 8/Church and Care

1. Eddy, *Retrospection*, p. 28.
2. Eddy, *Manual*, p. 17.
3. Eddy, *Message to The Mother Church for 1901*, p. 32.
4. Quoted in Peel, *Mary Baker Eddy I*, p. 288.
5. Eddy, *Manual*, p. 19.
6. Eddy, *Miscellaneous Writings*, pp. 144–45.
7. Clifford P. Smith, "An Interview with Mrs. Eddy," in *Permanence of The Mother Church* (Boston: Christian Science Publishing Society, 1972), p. 5.
8. Eddy, *Message for 1901*, p. 11.
9. Allison W. Phinney, Jr., "A Sermon from his personal God," *Christian Science Journal*, August 1984, p. 510.
10. See Erwin D. Canham, *Commitment to Freedom: The Story of The Christian Science Monitor* (Boston: Houghton Mifflin, 1958). See also Canham, *A Christian Scientist's Life*, and DeWitt John, *The Christian Science Way of Life* (Englewood Cliffs, N.J.: Prentice-Hall, 1962); Peel, *Encounter*, pp. 163–81; Stephen Gottschalk, *The Emergence of Christian Science in American Religious Life* (Berkeley and Los Angeles: University of California Press, 1973), pp. 259–74; Peel, *Mary Baker Eddy II*, pp. 183–84, and *Mary Baker Eddy III*, pp. 131–40, 255–56, 300–8, 329–30; *A Century of Christian Science Healing*, pp. 249–51; *Understanding Our Century*, ed. Earl W. Foell (Boston: Christian Science Publishing Society, 1984); *An Agenda for the 21st Century*, ed. Rushworth M. Kidder, foreword by Katherine Fanning (Cambridge, Mass.: MIT Press, 1987), pp. ix–xiii.
11. Norman Beasley, *The Continuing Spirit* (New York: Duell, Sloan and Pearce, 1956), pp. 100–110; *The Story of Christian Science Wartime Activities 1939–1946* (Boston: Christian Science Publishing Society, 1947); Peel, *Mary Baker Eddy III*, pp. 468–69 n. 2.
12. Eddy, *Science and Health*, p. 395.
13. The instruction is devoted as much to what the nurses are *not* to do as to what they *are* to do. They are not to stray beyond their assigned duty of providing cleanliness, comfort, and loving care of the patient's practical needs, and of maintaining an atmosphere of thought that is conducive to healing. The nurse must resist any temptation to diagnose a case, either medically or metaphysically.
14. There are at present 40 Christian Science nursing homes, several of them outside the United States. In addition there are 138 retirement homes for Christian Scientists and an undetermined number of facilities for temporary rest and study. See also *A Century of Christian Science Healing*, pp. 239–43.
15. Eddy, *Manual*, p. 49.
16. *Ecumenical Papers*, pp. 6–7.
17. See Peel, *Mary Baker Eddy III*, pp. 255, 468–69.
18. There are no official lists of these organizations, and their numbers wax and wane. The figures that follow are approximate, but they roughly represent the situation at the end of 1987. So far as could be ascertained at that time there are 26 such schools and camps, a few of them serving both functions.
19. The 1987 tally was 12 foundations with a variety of purposes, ranging from

financial assistance to Christian Science college students to support of residential and nursing homes.

20. The church has no record of businessmen's or businesswomen's clubs. Over the past forty years I have been invited to address several such clubs but have been too busy to accept their invitations and cannot now remember the cities from which the invitations came. From inquiries I have made of friends it appears that such groups tend to be somewhat ephemeral. For Eddy's lack of enthusiasm for these and other social clubs of Christian Scientists, see my *Mary Baker Eddy III*, pp. 226–27.

21. The Foundation for Biblical Research in Charlestown, New Hampshire, and the Longyear Foundation in Brookline, Massachusetts, are the only two such societies at present. The first was established in the mid-1960s to promote the study of "primitive Christianity," the Longyear society in the mid-1920s to gather and preserve historical materials of all sorts having to do with the early years of Christian Science.

22. The Longyear Foundation has done a certain amount of publishing, but for the most part this category is represented by books whose authors have had them privately printed.

23. Peel, *Mary Baker Eddy III*, p. 226.

24. Ibid., p. 225.

25. Eddy, *Manual*, p. 44.

Chapter 9/Spiritual Healing

1. Peel, *Spiritual Healing in a Scientific Age* (San Francisco: Harper and Row, 1987), p. viii; hereafter cited as *Spiritual Healing*.

2. During the past thirty years I have made a point of asking Christian Science friends and acquaintances who have had remarkable healings whether they have ever written a detailed account of these healings for publication in the Christian Science periodicals. I would say that about one in eight has done this, although most of them have given oral expression of their gratitude for these experiences at the Wednesday testimony meetings. It was only in 1985 that I finally realized that I myself had never given a written account of healings I had experienced. This omission was rectified by adding a chapter entitled "Personal Testament" to my book *Spiritual Healing*, then in preparation.

3. Benjamin O. Flower, *Christian Science As a Religious Belief and a Therapeutic Agent* (Boston: Twentieth Century Company, 1909), pp. 61–158; Frances Thurber Seal, *Christian Science in Germany* (Philadelphia: John C. Winston Press, 1931; reprinted by Longyear Foundation in 1977); Will Oursler, *The Healing Power of Faith* (New York: Hawthorn Books, 1957), pp. 101–12; Peel, *Encounter*, 1958, pp. 137–63, 214–22; *A Century of Christian Science Healing*, 1966; Peel, *Spiritual Healing*, 1987.

4. Lee Z. Johnson, "The Christian Science Committee on Publication: A Study of Group and Press Interaction." Ph.D. diss., Syracuse University, 1963.

5. Geoffrey Hoyland, *The Resurrection Pattern* (London: Gerald Duckworth, 1947), p. 67.

6. W. Bonser, quoted in Rex Gardner, "Miracles of Healing in Anglo-Celtic Northumbria . . . ," *British Medical Journal*, 24–31 December 1983, p. 1928.

7. Ibid.

8. Rex Gardner, *Healing Miracles* (London: Darton, Longman and Todd, 1986), p. 4.

9. Ibid., pp. 25–27.

10. Eddy, *Science and Health*, p. 313.

11. Ibid., p. 55.

12. The Christian Science Committee on Publication plays a crucial role in keeping Christian Scientists aware of their legal responsibilities and rights in regard to their reliance on spiritual means of healing. More than any other arm of the church except the *Christian Science Monitor*, the Committee on Publication is in touch with the medical profession, public health officials, legislators, the courts, the press, and representatives of other churches—including the ecumenical and spiritual healing interests they may share with the last-named group. The *Manual* assigns to the Committee on Publication the duty of correcting public misconceptions of Christian Science and the injustices that may follow from such misunderstandings. But from the outset Eddy saw this corrective mission as necessitating the committee's involvement and advice in practical situations requiring better mutual understanding between Christian Scientists and society at large.

13. A few names familiar to those acquainted with Christian Science history are Francis J. Fluno, Alfred Baker, W. F. W. Wilding (British), Edmund F. Burton, Walton Hubbard, and John M. Tutt. During the past fifty years I have met and talked with a number of other less prominent figures who have become Christian Scientists at some point in their medical careers, as well as one or two individuals who have left Christian Science to take up a career of medical practice or research.

14. Eddy, *Science and Health*, pp. 164, 444.

15. Eddy, *First Church and Miscellany*, p. 4; *Manual*, p. 48.

16. Thomas C. Johnsen, "Christian Scientists and the Medical Profession: A Historical Perspective," *Medical Heritage*, January/February 1986, pp. 71–77.

17. A not untypical editorial comment was that of the New York *Morning Telegraph*, quoted in Edward Kimball, Clifford Smith, and Septimus Hanna, *Christian Science and Legislation* (Boston: Christian Science Publishing Society, 1909): "It is this cumulative evidence [of Christian Science healing] that gives weight to the belief that one can be healed by faith."

18. Mark Twain, *Christian Science* (New York: Harper, 1907), p. 80.

19. Eddy, *Science and Health*, p. 66.

20. Johnsen, "Christian Scientists," p. 75; cf. Peel, *Spiritual Healing*, pp. 41–42.

21. Eddy, *Rudimental Divine Science*, p. 2.

22. Eddy, *Science and Health*, p. 150.

23. See Peel, *Encounter*, pp. xii, 137–63, 214–25.

24. Stefan Zweig, *Mental Healers: Mesmer, Eddy, Freud* (New York: Viking, 1932), p. 246.

25. Michael Drury, *Every Whit Whole: The Adventure of Spiritual Healing* (New York: Dodd, Mead, 1978), p. 85.

26. *Commonwealth vs. Sheridan*, 1967.

27. *New England Journal of Medicine,* 14 February 1974, pp. 401, 402. Quoted in Peel, *Spiritual Healing,* pp. 41–42 and 202 n. 13.

28. *Letters of William James,* ed. Henry James (Boston: Atlantic Monthly Press, 1920), 2:66–72.

29. Johnsen, "Christian Scientists," p. 75; see Peel, *Spiritual Healing,* pp. 125–26.

30. *Cincinnati Enquirer,* 4 April 1987.

31. Allison W. Phinney, Jr., "There is a battle at the crossroads," *Christian Science Sentinel,* 6 July 1987. See also Phinney, "Spirituality or Materialism: Crossroads for Humanity," *Christian Science Monitor,* 29 August 1983.

32. Lois O'Brien, "Prayer's not a gamble," *U.S. News & World Report,* 28 April 1986.

33. Phinney, "There is a battle."

Chapter 10/Decision at the Crossroads

1. Eddy, *Science and Health,* p. 239.

2. Ibid., pp. 35, 444.

3. Eddy, *Miscellaneous Writings,* pp. 86, 87.

4. Eddy, *Science and Health,* p. 243.

5. Eddy, *Miscellaneous Writings,* p. 389.

6. Stephen Gottschalk, "Resuming the Dialogue with Christian Science," *Christian Century,* 17 December 1986, pp. 1146–48.

7. Eddy, *First Church and Miscellany,* p. 162.

8. Quoted in Peel, *Mary Baker Eddy III,* p. 223.

9. Eddy, *Miscellaneous Writings,* pp. 110–11.

10. Eddy, *Science and Health,* p. 134.

11. Ibid., pp. 15–16.

12. Some of these can be found in *A Century of Christian Science Healing* and *The Story of Christian Science Wartime Activities 1939–1946.* Others are scattered in testimonies and articles in Christian Science periodicals through the years since 1946 or in the historical files of The Mother Church.

13. Arthur Schlesinger, Sr., *The Rise of the City* (New York: Macmillan, 1933), p. 338.

14. Peel, *Mary Baker Eddy III,* p. 59.

15. Eddy, *Rudimental Divine Science,* p. 2.

16. Peel, *Mary Baker Eddy III,* pp. 15–16.

17. Ibid., p. 39.

18. Leslie Weatherhead, *Psychology, Religion and Healing* (London: Hodder and Stoughton, 1951), p. 195.

19. Helen Wood Bauman, Robert Peel, Peter J. Henniker-Heaton, *Mary Baker Eddy: Discoverer, Founder, Leader* (Boston: Christian Science Publishing Society, 1977), p. 30.

20. Helen A. Nixon, letter in *Christian Science Sentinel* 11, no. 17, 26 December 1908.

21. Messer, *Family in the Making,* p. 354.

22. Eddy, *Science and Health,* p. 249. For the background of Helen Nixon,

daughter of Methodist Bishop Andrews of New York and longtime Christian Science practitioner and teacher of Christian Science, see Peel, *Mary Baker Eddy III*, pp. 386–87 n. 94. In 1932, still active, she endorsed my application for membership in The Mother Church and encouraged my early academic research into the history of Christian Science.

23. Interview with Clara Barton in *New York American*, 6 January 1908.

24. See Peel, *Mary Baker Eddy III*, pp. 312–13.

25. Ibid., p. 497 n. 74.

26. Frederick Dixon, "Mary Baker Eddy," *Outlook* (London), reprinted in *Editorial Comments on the Life and Work of Mary Baker Eddy* (Boston: Christian Science Publishing Society, 1911), pp. 3–8.

27. Eddy, *First Church and Miscellany*, p. 355.

28. *Boston Sunday Post*, 29 March 1914, p. 39.

29. Eddy, *Science and Health*, p. xi.

30. Since membership numbers are unobtainable, calculations must be based on the numbers of churches and the evidence of attendance at services.

31. Peel, *Mary Baker Eddy III*, p. 223.

32. Eddy, *Miscellaneous Writings*, p. 200.

33. Peel, *Encounter*, pp. 202–3.

34. Eddy, *Miscellaneous Writings*, p. 148.

35. Eddy, *Manual*, p. 104.

36. Eddy, *First Church and Miscellany*, p. 230.

37. Robert Frost, *The Road Not Taken* (New York: Henry Holt, 1915), p. 271.

Index

Health/Medicine and the Faith Traditions

HEALTH AND MEDICINE IN THE ANGLICAN TRADITION
David H. Smith

HEALTH AND MEDICINE IN THE CATHOLIC TRADITION
Richard A. McCormick

HEALTH AND MEDICINE IN THE CHRISTIAN SCIENCE TRADITION
Robert Peel

HEALTH AND MEDICINE IN THE ISLAMIC TRADITION
Fazlur Rahman

HEALTH AND MEDICINE IN THE JEWISH TRADITION
David M. Feldman

HEALTH AND MEDICINE IN THE LUTHERAN TRADITION
Martin E. Marty

HEALTH AND MEDICINE IN THE METHODIST TRADITION
E. Brooks Holifield

HEALTH AND MEDICINE IN THE REFORMED TRADITION
Kenneth L. Vaux